PRAISE FO

I WILL PROTECT YOU: A TRUE STORY OF TWINS WHO SURVIVED AUSCHWITZ

"A well-written memoir, a gripping story of prejudice, hatred, horror, and forgiveness. It belongs on every shelf of books for young readers on the Nazi Holocaust and of books attacking racism." —David A. Adler, award-winning author of *The Number on My Grandfather's Arm, We Remember the Holocaust*, and many other books

"Emotional and captivating; this story is a great tool for a younger audience wishing to understand the harsh realities faced by twin children in concentration camps." —Andrew Aydin, National Book Award–winning and #1 *New York Times* bestselling creator and coauthor of *March*

"Few Holocaust survivors have had Eva Mozes Kor's impact....Read this work and meet a person you will never forget with a story that is worth telling and retelling." —Michael Berenbaum, award-winning author; professor of Jewish Studies, American Jewish University; and former director of the United States Holocaust Memorial Museum's Holocaust Research Institute

"Harrowing but ultimately redemptive...a story of irrational hope and courage." —Mark Long, *New York Times* bestselling author *The Silence of Our Friends*

"One of the best Holocaust memoirs I have ever read (and I have read many).... This book illuminates the human spirit and proves that even in the very worst circumstances, kindness can be found. I am a better person for having read this book." —Lesléa Newman, award-winning author of *Gittel's Journey: An Ellis Island Story*

"This riveting eyewitness account of the Nazi horrors, written in a way that a sympathetic young reader can understand, is needed now more than ever." —David Small, National Book Award finalist and #1 *New York Times* bestselling author of *Stitches*

"A compelling story of survival." —*Booklist*

"Bright and compelling, Eva invites young readers to plant flowers of knowledge, love, and acceptance in their own minds.... Moving and informative; a powerful resource for Holocaust education." —*Kirkus Reviews*

"Powerful.... Unflinching in its first-person telling, the narrative is carried by its narrator's passionate conviction, per an afterword, that 'memories will provide the necessary fuel to light the way to hope.'" —*Publishers Weekly*

I Will Protect You

A TRUE STORY OF TWINS WHO SURVIVED AUSCHWITZ

I Will Protect You

A TRUE STORY OF TWINS
WHO SURVIVED AUSCHWITZ

As Told by EVA MOZES KOR

Written by DANICA DAVIDSON

LITTLE, BROWN AND COMPANY
New York Boston

Little, Brown and Company
Hachette Book Group
1290 Avenue of the Americas, New York, NY 10104
Visit us at LBYR.com

Originally published in hardcover and ebook by Little, Brown and Company in April 2022
First Trade Paperback Edition: October 2023

Little, Brown and Company is a division of Hachette Book Group, Inc.
The Little, Brown name and logo are trademarks of
Hachette Book Group, Inc.

The publisher is not responsible for websites (or their content) that are not owned by
the publisher.

Little, Brown and Company books may be purchased in bulk for business, educational,
or promotional use. For information, please contact your local bookseller or the
Hachette Book Group Special Markets Department at special.markets@hbgusa.com.

The Library of Congress cataloged the hardcover edition as follows:
Names: Kor, Eva Mozes. | Davidson, Danica, author.
Title: I will protect you : a true story of twins who survived Auschwitz / as told by
Eva Mozes Kor ; written by Danica Davidson.
Description: First edition. | New York : Little, Brown and Company, 2022. | Audience:
Ages 8–12 | Summary: "A memoir of a young girl's childhood in wartime Romania,
unlikely survival as a 'Mengele twin' subjected to cruel Nazi medical experiments in
Auschwitz, and postwar journey to forgiveness"— Provided by publisher.
Identifiers: LCCN 2021047481 | ISBN 9780316460637 (hardcover) |
ISBN 9780316460620 (ebook)
Subjects: LCSH: Kor, Eva Mozes—Juvenile literature. | Zeiger, Miriam Mozes,
1935–1993—Juvenile literature. | Jews—Persecutions—Romania—Porţ—Juvenile
literature. | Jewish children in the Holocaust—Romania—Biography—Juvenile
literature. | Holocaust, Jewish (1939–1945)—Romania—Sălaj—Personal
narratives—Juvenile literature. | Twins—Biography—Juvenile literature. | Human
experimentation in medicine—Juvenile literature. | Auschwitz (Concentration
camp)—Juvenile literature. | Porţ (Romania)—Biography—Juvenile literature. |
CYAC: Holocaust survivors—Biography—Juvenile literature.
Classification: LCC DS135.R73 K66 2022 | DDC 940.53/180922
[B]—dc23/eng/20211006
LC record available at https://lccn.loc.gov/2021047481

ISBNs: 978-0-316-46060-6 (pbk.),
978-0-316-46062-0 (ebook)

Printed in the United States of America

LSC-C

Printing 1, 2023

In loving memory of Eva Mozes Kor
(1934–2019)

Who knew a world of learning, love,
justice, and healing is a better world
than one of ignorance, hate, cruelty, and
extremism.
Who especially wanted her message to
become a book for kids so they can be
the leaders of a better day.

"I want my time on this earth to count for
something."
—Eva Mozes Kor

I Will Protect You

A TRUE STORY OF TWINS WHO SURVIVED AUSCHWITZ

CHAPTER ONE

Trouble at School

The other kids were up to something. My identical twin sister, Miriam, and I watched as boys tiptoed across our one-room schoolhouse with little bird eggs in their hands. Grinning, they laid the eggs on the teacher's chair as if it were a nest. Then they sneaked back to their seats and sat calmly, like perfect little angels.

None of the forty-four students said anything. It had been a long winter in the Transylvanian mountains, and now the warm spring air blew gently into the classroom. It meant a day of flowers and sunlight, and I couldn't wait for what was to come. It felt like a day that promised fun and happiness.

Our teacher, Mrs. Margit, was wearing the perfect dress for spring. It was white with soft pink and yellow flowers. My mama loved dressing Miriam and me in matching dresses that she had specially made by a tailor in the city. So I knew a thing or two about clothes. The other girls at school wore long skirts with scarves covering their heads, and the boys wore trousers and shirts.

"Now, class," Mrs. Margit began, turning to face us and backing into her chair. She hadn't noticed the eggs, and when she sat on them, they crunched louder than a scream. Mrs. Margit leapt to her feet and looked behind her. What a mess! Our village did not have any electricity or running water, and it would take a lot of scrubbing to get the eggs out of that pretty dress.

A boy pointed his finger like a dagger at Miriam and me. "The dirty Jews did it!" he shouted.

The kids we played with looked at us like we were

snakes: maybe dangerous and definitely not human. Miriam and I were the only two Jews in the class, and ours was the only Jewish family in the entire village.

"Did you?" Mrs. Margit demanded angrily, glaring at Miriam and me.

"No, Madame Teacher, no!" we exclaimed. Everyone had seen what really had happened, and I hoped another kid would tell her the truth. They all knew us, Miriam and Eva Mozes, and they knew we wouldn't be mean to the teacher like that. I looked at my best friend, Luci. Miriam and I helped decorate Luci's Christmas tree, and she came over to our house to play.

"Yes, they did!" another child shouted. "We saw them!"

"Punish them!"

Luci looked down and said nothing.

Mrs. Margit ordered Miriam and me to the front of the room, facing the class. She savagely hurled a pile of corn kernels onto the classroom floor. "Kneel!" she commanded.

The kernels were hard and small, and they bit into our bare knees like pebbles with sharp edges. The longer we had to kneel there, the more it hurt. Mrs. Margit forced us to stay there for a whole hour.

While we knelt, the class made faces at us. Even with Miriam there beside me, I felt so alone. Why did everyone hate us?

Our schoolbooks were filled with anti-Jewish ideas. We had a math question during class one day: "If you had five Jews, and you killed three Jews, how many Jews would you have left?" The real answer was two. But the question seemed to suggest "two too many."

One by one, the other kids turned against us. A girl who used to play a game trying to tell Miriam and me apart started calling us dirty, smelly Jews. A boy who never used to bother us threw us down into the dirt. The more the other kids learned to hate us, the more passionate about their hatred they became.

One night not long before, the whole village had come to the school after class to see a movie. I'd never seen one before, so I was excited. We called it a jumping picture. Standing there with my sisters and parents, we watched images move along the wall. The movie was called something like *How to Catch and Kill a Jew*.

The movie showed men with guns. Instead of hunting animals for food, these hunters were hunting Jews for sport. A Jewish father and son were running from the hunters. Shots were fired. The hunters dragged away the Jewish bodies. They killed Jewish people simply for being Jewish. The movie was over.

Everyone watching was stunned. But as more anti-Jewish books and movies came out, such images became a common thing to see, and the people got used to this antisemitism. They started to agree with it more. Even the people who didn't hate Jews, like my friend Luci, wouldn't raise their voices to help us.

It was 1941. Miriam and I were seven years old. We had no power. And people hated us.

Miriam and I felt so alone. But in a larger sense, we weren't. Millions of Jews had suffered for about two thousand years because of antisemitism—the hatred, fear, and violence directed toward Jewish people simply because they are Jewish. Antisemitism has taken on different forms over the centuries. In the Middle Ages,

Jews were banned from countries like France, Spain, and England. False stories were repeated that Jews murdered Christian children and drank their blood and that Jews poisoned wells to spread the plague. There was no evidence for this, but people believed it. During the Spanish Inquisition, which began in the 1400s, religious rulers believed they were doing holy work by forcing Jews to convert to Christianity and killing or expelling those who refused.

Even in modern times there were pogroms, where people would massacre groups of Jews.

Usually the country's government was behind it or let it happen. In the late nineteenth and twentieth centuries, many people realized that the stories about Jews spreading the plague and drinking blood were superstitious and ignorant beliefs, but the anti-Jewish thoughts morphed into something new. People were putting more faith in science, so antisemites came up with the idea that Jews were naturally evil based on their race. *I'm not ignorant for hating Jews,* they'd say. *I'm being scientific!*

To make things worse, a document called *The Protocols of the Elders of Zion* came out in 1903 in Russia and was sold around the world. The book claimed to be proof that powerful Jews were plotting to control the world through evil means. It was probably published by people massacring Jews, as an excuse to murder their neighbors. It was easy to prove that the document was fake and had been copied from earlier documents, including some that had nothing to do with Jews. But for people who wanted an enemy, it was just what they needed. It gave them "evidence" to say that fighting Jews was not only scientific but moral.

My classroom was full of little warriors, ready to do the right thing because they had been told it was the right thing. They grew up in a world where some churches still taught that it was holy to hate Jews. A world where some politicians talked about Jews as if we were the enemy of the people. Like a lot of adults, my classmates never questioned it or thought they should dig a little deeper.

As we had on so many other days after being bullied at school, Miriam and I ran home, crying.

"Mama!" I called, slamming open the door.

"Yes, Eva?" my mama said. "Yes. Calm down." I couldn't calm down. It was all so unfair!

Hearing what my classmates and Mrs. Margit had done made Mama cry, too. She held us close, whispering, "Children, I am so sorry. We are Jews, and we just have to take it. There is nothing we can do."

I always looked to Mama for comfort, but hearing this didn't soothe me at all. I wanted to march back to school and hurt Mrs. Margit, hurt her the way she'd hurt me. Of course I couldn't. Mrs. Margit was a grown-up, and grown-ups got away with everything. But then I wondered, *Why can't Mama take a stand?*

Papa was out working in the fields of our farm. When he got home, we told him the same story.

"Just say your prayers and ask God to help us," Papa said. That was his usual response to any problem.

My knees still hurt from the corn kernels. I never wanted to go back to that scary school again! I wished I could learn with my big sisters, Edit and Aliz. They were too old for the village school, so Mama had a tutor live in our house and teach them. Papa said girls didn't

8

need that much education, but Mama disagreed, and she won. The tutor was Jewish, too, and I'd learned some German words from her.

Even when the world outside was cruel, Mama tried to keep a loving home. She sang us songs and told us stories. She cooked delicious food from our farm and our gardens, and she tried to live by the words of an embroidered message she kept framed in the kitchen. The embroidery said: *Your mind is like a garden. Plant flowers so weeds can't grow.*

Although Mama was very gentle, she did tell me the hair-raising story of Little Red Riding Hood. A girl in a rose-red hood went to visit her grandmother in the forest, where it was dark, deep, and so far from home. In the grandmother's house, an old woman waited for Little Red. An old, strange-looking woman with big eyes and even bigger teeth.

"What big eyes you have," said Little Red Riding Hood.

"All the better to see you with," said the grandmother, who was really a wolf in disguise.

"What big hands you have," said Little Red Riding Hood.

"All the better to hug you with," said the wolf, his claws ready to attack.

"And what big teeth you have," said Little Red Riding Hood.

"All the better to eat you with!" And he leapt down and swallowed Little Red Riding Hood whole.

A wolf came near my family's farm during the winters to attack our livestock, so I already knew to fear wolves. But the scariest part of the story was the wolf's trick. He fooled the girl into thinking he was her sweet, safe grandmother when he was really a dangerous beast. At times, I felt like Little Red Riding Hood. She could tell something was wrong, but she couldn't figure it out in time. And look what happened to her.

CHAPTER TWO

Trouble at Home

At school I was all wrong because I was Jewish. At home I felt all wrong, too. That was because I was a girl, and Papa would tell me, "You should have been a boy."

It had to do with Papa's very strict religious beliefs. Back then only boys could say the Kaddish, the Jewish prayer for the dead. Papa wanted a boy who could some-day say the Kaddish for him. Papa did not complain that my sisters, Edit, Aliz, and Miriam, were girls. But I was the youngest, and he had hoped his last child would be a boy.

None of us were as religious as Papa, but he made the rules in the household. If a knife fell on the floor, this was a crisis for him because he had to do rituals to make it kosher again. Keeping kosher meant we followed strict Jewish food laws. Papa was also very concerned that we did the right things on the Sabbath, which we called Shabbos. From sundown Friday to sundown Saturday, we were forbidden to do any work. Papa had us tie our handkerchiefs around our wrists if we needed to wipe our noses because carrying something was considered work.

With Papa being as unchanging as he was, and with me speaking out as much I as did, we didn't exactly see eye to eye. And I hated being told I was wrong for being a girl! I'd argue with Papa and act out, and that got me in trouble. Sometimes when I misbehaved, he'd drag me into the cellar to sit there and think about what I'd done. The madder I got at him, the madder he got at me.

It didn't help that he treated my other sisters better. I didn't see him punishing Edit or Aliz the way he did me. And he loved sweet, quiet Miriam dearly. He'd cuddle her on his lap and tell her stories about Palestine, the Jewish homeland, which was originally called Eretz Israel or Judea. Miriam loved Papa back. It seemed like she could never do anything wrong in his eyes, just like I could never do anything right.

My big sister Edit, who was four years older, would egg me on to bug Papa. That must have been amusing to her. Silly little Eva, getting in trouble with Papa again!

But Edit also would play with Miriam and me, so I liked her. I had a harder time getting along with Aliz. Aliz was two years older and thought Miriam and I were babies. And she was so beautiful. She was the only one of us who didn't have any freckles and never gained weight, no matter what she ate. This made it easy to envy her. She was very talented at drawing. Whole worlds came to life on the page when she had paper and a pencil.

Mama and Papa had had an arranged marriage, which was common where we lived. Friends of Papa's had gone looking for a woman for him to marry, and Mama and her family had agreed to it. Papa was very happy with his farm and his prayers, but Mama wanted a more exciting life than living in the country. She was well educated for a woman back then, and she never had a problem that I was a girl.

Sometimes she and Papa argued loudly, and I would hear the scary word *divorce*. But they always stayed together.

As things got worse outside our home, they got worse inside it, too. Mama and Papa stayed by the radio at night, talking to each other in Yiddish. I didn't think that was fair because we kids didn't know Yiddish. It was the secret language of parents, keeping us out.

I could hear some of what was said on the radio, though. I heard the name Adolf Hitler. I heard the word *Nazis*. The Nazis were a political group in Germany that had come to power. Their leader, Adolf Hitler, wanted to take over Europe. He and his Nazis hated Jews so much that it was a main part of their party's platform. Some people supported the Nazis because they also hated Jews. Some supported the Nazis because they wanted to improve Germany's standing in the world, and if antisemitism was part of the politics, so be it. In just a few years since they started their military aggression, the Nazis had taken over Austria,

Czechoslovakia, Poland, France, Belgium, the Netherlands, Greece, and Yugoslavia and invaded the western part of the Soviet Union. And they kept expanding, getting closer and closer to the village of Portz, where we lived. *The Protocols of the Elders of Zion*, the made-up document about evil Jewish power, was being taught as true in Nazi classrooms. On the radio I heard Hitler screaming about killing Jews.

I wanted to know what was going on. But I always got the same sort of answer from my parents. "Don't worry about Hitler—he and his Nazis won't get this far," they took turns telling me. "The Nazis won't come all the way to our village of Portz for a mere six Jews and their tutor. They have more important things to do. We are fine."

I could see on a map that our Romanian village of Portz was in Hungary, in Eastern Europe. With the Nazis on the move, it didn't seem far-fetched that they would reach us. It made me very angry that my parents weren't listening when I kept telling them my fears.

After classmates harassed Miriam and me at school, some older, braver kids decided to harass all of us at home. Teenagers circled our house like wolves, shouting about "dirty Jews." They threw tomatoes at our house.

Sometimes they threw rocks, which shattered the windows into crystal shards.

Then adult villagers joined the teenage boys. But instead of telling the boys to go home, the village grown-ups helped them yell and throw objects.

"Crazy pigs!" they shouted at us.

Sometimes the villagers stayed for days and it wasn't safe to go outside.

I couldn't take it anymore. I confronted Papa. "Papa," I begged. "Please go out and make them stop!"

I felt so much anger inside me, swelling.

"Eva, you are quite a spoiled child!" Papa yelled at me. "You just don't seem to want to understand." Then he went back to his usual speech: "We are Jews. We just have to take it."

"I think we should leave," I argued. Papa always said I had a big mouth. He didn't mean it as a good thing. "It's not safe to stay here."

Papa shook his head. The look on his face said, *What does a child know?*

I knew that the walls were closing in on us. And that no one was listening to me.

CHAPTER THREE

Fleeing
in the Night

"Eva, Miriam, wake up!" Papa called.

I slowly came out of a deep sleep. The whole house was dark. It was before sunrise, and there wasn't even a candle burning. Mama and Papa stood by the bed that Miriam and I shared. Even if I couldn't really see their faces in the darkness, I could feel how tense they were. It was the fall of 1943. Miriam and I were nine.

"Get dressed," Papa said. "Quietly. Put on your warm

clothes, your boots. Do not light a candle," he quickly added because that was what I was about to do. It would be hard to get dressed without light. "Be very, very quiet."

"What are we doing?" I asked.

"Eva, please, just do as you're told," Papa said in a typical Papa response.

Miriam and I got up sleepily, pulled our clothes on, and walked into the kitchen. Our older sisters were already there and dressed. There were no candles lit here, either, but some red embers gleamed faintly in the potbelly stove. It was too dark to see Mama's embroidery.

"Children," Papa said, "we are going to try to get over the Romanian border. We have decided the time has come when we must leave. You are to follow us. Make no noise."

Lately things had gotten worse in Hungary, and not just for Jews. Even though my family spoke Hungarian, I lived in a village of Romanians. It was confusing like this because sometimes my village was part of Hungary, and sometimes it was part of Romania. The leader of Hungary had teamed up with the Nazis, and the Hungarian

Army had been taught to hate Romanians the same way it was taught to hate Jews.

Hungary wasn't the only country to team up with the Nazis. Other nations were either fighting the Nazis (called the Allies) or teaming up with the Nazis (called the Axis). The United States, England, France, and the Soviet Union were the most important Allies. Germany, Italy, and Japan were the Axis powers, later joined by Hungary, Romania, and Bulgaria, among others.

As quietly as we could, we sneaked out of our home. We were going to leave behind everything I'd ever known—our little house, our big farm. The view of the trees and the mountains outside my bedroom window. My best friend, Luci. It was scary, but it was also all right. We could be safer if we got out.

I really wished Papa would tell us more. Would we just camp out on the other side of the Romanian border?

Maybe we could go to Palestine, where Papa's brother Aaron had moved when I was a baby. Before that, Uncle Aaron and Papa had been arrested on fake charges having to do with their taxes and thrown in jail for a little while. They were really arrested for being Jewish. That was why Uncle Aaron left Europe.

Back then, Papa was all for following Uncle Aaron to Palestine. But Mama said it would be too hard to move there with small children. That new name, Palestine, came from the Roman Empire, which had conquered the land and cast many Jews out, and it appeared the land had been renamed to erase our connection to it.

During World War II, Palestine belonged to the British. Jews fleeing to Palestine to escape Hitler were not finding it easy. Many Jews weren't allowed in. Jews who tried to escape to other countries were often turned away. If they couldn't escape to Great Britain, Switzerland, the United States, Canada, or elsewhere, the Jews had to return to Europe, where the Nazis were waiting for them.

Would that happen to us, too?

Once outside our house, Papa walked in front, guiding us in the chilly and windswept night. We girls were behind him, single file. Mama was at the back of the line, watching over us.

We headed for the very back of our property, toward

the railroad tracks. If we followed the tracks like a map, they would take us over the border where we wanted to go.

Papa moved to unlatch the gate at the end of our property. A shout made him freeze. "*Stop!*" yelled an angry voice. A group of teenage boys stepped out of the darkness, pointing guns.

"If you take another step, I'll shoot!" one hissed.

It was just like the film we'd seen in school! None of us took a step. I grabbed Miriam's hand as tightly as I could.

The boys made us turn around and go back. I felt the gun pointed at us the whole time.

They led us all the way into our house and slammed the doors.

CHAPTER FOUR

Leaving Home

Nothing was the same after that. Edit and Aliz's tutor had to leave, and we knew that if we tried to escape again, we would be caught and sent back. Or worse.

Miriam and I still went to school, and it was still agony. In much of Europe, Jews had been banned from attending school with Christian children. This did not happen to us. The anti-Jewish rules had been enacted gradually. Early on, Hitler told people they could no longer shop at places owned by Jews.

There were book burnings. Jews were forbidden to work on newspapers, so they could not tell their stories. Jewish-owned businesses had to close.

Soon Jews could not hire non-Jews to work for them. They could not marry non-Jews.

Eventually Jews were banned even from owning pets! More and more, Jews were stripped of all rights. And war continued to spread.

What could I do? At home I liked to escape into books, especially adventure stories about brave girls who saved the day. But sometimes even the books couldn't help me feel better. The villagers had learned about our escape plan, and that made them even angrier at us. They came more often, yelling at us and throwing more tomatoes and rocks.

And then there was Mama. Poor Mama! After our failed escape, she got very sick with typhoid fever, and it lasted for months. There were no doctors in our village.

As chilling as things were in the outside world, watching Mama go from strong to weak was even worse. She couldn't even turn in the bed. Papa nursed her tenderly, slowly helping her get better. I wasn't used to seeing him be so gentle with her. As much as they might sometimes fight, we were all still a family.

Miriam's and my tenth birthday came on January 31, 1944. Normally a birthday meant celebrating and delicious cake. Not this year. As the weeks went by, Mama began to sit up in bed and move around more. That was a good enough birthday gift for me! I hoped our next birthday would be even better!

The Nazis invaded Hungary in March 1944, and now we had to all wear yellow Star of David patches on our clothes. It was a Nazi law so that everyone could know who was Jewish. But forcing Jews to wear different clothing was nothing new—it had been done for centuries, in different times and places. It started in the Middle East more than a thousand years earlier, when the law said Jews had to wear yellow badges. In 1215 in Europe, the Pope's Fourth Council of the Lateran dictated that Jews had to dress differently from Christians.

The Nazis weren't original—they were only building on old antisemitic practices.

But things took a new and terrifying twist later that spring.

It started with someone pounding on the door. Two Hungarian policemen, called gendarmes, were standing on our porch. Were we being arrested?

"Get your belongings!" one of the gendarmes ordered. "Gather them up. You are going to be moved to a ghetto for two weeks. Then you'll be sent to a labor camp. You have two hours to pack!"

A labor camp was not like a camp where kids go in the summer. It was a place where everyone worked without pay. The Nazis could have just called it what it was: *slavery*.

Papa, my sisters, and I packed clothing, bedding, and food so Mama could rest. Outside, the gendarmes waited for us. They had guns and a buggy to put us in.

Villagers came out of their homes to gawk as we were taken away. I stared at their faces. They weren't throwing tomatoes or rocks at us. They weren't yelling at us. No. But they weren't standing up for us, either.

There was not a single person there to say, "Wait a minute. Is this really the best thing to do?"

I saw children from school.

I saw men who earned their money by working on Papa's farm.

I saw people I had known my entire life just standing there. Standing and watching.

Doing nothing. Saying nothing.

And then we were coming up to Luci's house. Luci, my best friend! Dear, sweet Luci, she'd have to say something! Or—or—or her father would! Yes, Luci's papa was the minister of the one church in Portz, and he was greatly respected. He knew I was not the dirty, evil creature from the anti-Jewish books and movies. I was a regular girl like any other girl who just wanted to live a normal life.

But Luci's papa did not come out and help us. And when we passed Luci's home, I saw her standing in front of it. Her eyes were down, the same way they'd been at school when Miriam and I had been blamed for the prank.

She wouldn't even say goodbye.

CHAPTER FIVE

The Ghetto

The gendarmes took us to a field with a barbed wire fence around it. There were thousands of Jews inside who looked poor and frightened. I was amazed. In my village, there had been maybe one hundred people, so I'd never seen such a crowd.

A river split the ghetto into two parts. The families had set up little tents. There was one brick building in the background, but I bet Jews weren't allowed in there. It would be too nice.

So this was a *ghetto*. According to my parents, ghettos were sealed-off places where Jews were forced to live. They could be killed for leaving. Like making Jews wear special clothing, ghettos had been used in different times and places to keep Jews away from everyone else. By putting us in a ghetto, the Nazis were just copying history again.

At some points in history, my parents told me, Jews have been able to turn their ghettos into nicer places. I could quickly see that this wasn't going to be true for this ghetto. It looked as if the Nazis had just sloppily thrown something together to stick all the local Jews in.

A well-built man in a Nazi uniform came out of the brick building, his beefy hands on his hips, looking at us and smiling. He was the commandant, the man in charge of this ghetto. He lived in the brick house.

While Mama rested, Papa, my sisters, and I made a tent out of blankets. The commandant watched us, his hands still on his hips, his face still smiling. When we were done, he exclaimed, "Isn't that great? Look at the Children of Israel living in their tents like the days of Moses!" He laughed some more, thinking he was very clever. No one joined him.

A little later it started to rain. While we all ducked for cover into the tent, the commandant had other ideas.

"Tear your tents down and build them on the other side of the river!" he ordered through his loudspeaker.

So we pulled down our tent, got all our stuff, and made our way to the other side of the river. All the other Jews did the same. Water splattered from the heavens, drenching us. Everything was soaked through. The commandant couldn't stop laughing.

This was something new. In school and in the village, everyone had been very self-righteous in attacking Jews, thinking they were doing the right thing to make the world better. But the commandant just thought all this was hilarious.

When the rain ended, we crawled back outside. Drops of water hung on the barbed wire, making it glint like knife blades caught in the sun. All the Jews stuck close to their families. We only had to stay here for two weeks. We could handle anything for two weeks, we told ourselves.

With this hope we continued our day-to-day lives. But I was so scared, especially for Mama's sake. Being soaked in rain and living like this was not helping her get better. The ghetto wasn't like home, where I could just escape into books. It wasn't really a good place to play games, either, and I didn't know any of the other kids there. One of Miriam's and my favorite games back home was asking people whether they could tell us apart. We could even trick family members. The only one we could never trick was Papa. He could always see right through me.

For a while, the Nazis in charge of the ghetto left my family alone. But I watched as they went to other families, demanding to speak with the head of the household. They meant the husband or father. They would take the man away to the brick building. When the man returned, he was often hurt and on a stretcher.

One day the shadow of Nazi guards fell across our little tent. They demanded to see Papa. Privately.

There was no way to fight them. They took Papa away to the big brick building, where they would do whatever they wanted with him. The Nazis shut the door, sealing him in. Sealing us out.

All we could do was wait. That was its own form of torture.

CHAPTER SIX

"Where Are Your Gold and Silver?"

The Nazis brought Papa back on a stretcher, a broken man. His body was streaked with bloody marks and purple with bruises.

"Papa! Papa!" we cried as the Nazis roughly dropped his body to the ground. We circled around him, checking his wounds, wanting to know what had happened. First Mama had been so weak, and now Papa could barely move.

Papa's hands shook. That was when I saw that all of his fingernails had turned black. The Nazis had also whipped and beaten him.

Slowly, slowly, Papa was able to tell us what happened. The Nazis had heard we were wealthy. Nazis seemed to think Jews were always rich, so they were taking one man per family away and torturing him until he told them where his wealth was. Then the Nazis would steal from him and return him to his family.

Almost all our money went into the land we owned. We were what's known as land-poor. But the Nazis did not torture Papa for his land. They'd already taken us from our land, so they could steal our farm whenever they wanted. No, they wanted more. They figured that Papa had hidden gold and silver on the farm, and they wanted to know exactly where to look.

When Papa said there was no hidden gold or silver, they didn't believe him. Along with being taught that Jews were always rich from evil doings, Nazis were taught that Jews always lied. Papa said the only silver he had was in his silver candleholders. Every Shabbos we lit candles to celebrate. This was a very important Jewish ritual.

The Nazis didn't want candleholders. They wanted treasure troves of wealth that didn't exist. And when Papa told them the truth, they forced his fingers into candle flames. While Papa cried out and tried to protect his poor hand, they doubled down in their questioning. *Where is your gold? Where is your silver? Tell us, you dirty Jew!* And when he still said there was no other silver, they burned his toes in the same flames.

People had been tortured in the Middle Ages to get them to confess, and here the Nazis were, continuing the same practice. When Papa continued to tell them the truth, they beat and whipped him.

Finally, they realized they weren't going to get anything out of Papa. Furious that he'd wasted their time, they carried him out of the brick building. They had other families to confront.

For about three days Papa could barely move. Miriam and I didn't know what to do.

His bruises changed color, and his whip marks slowly began to heal.

Because she was the oldest, Edit started cooking meals. Papa helped her. Scared of running out of food, we began eating a single meal of beans each day. Eating beans day after day was pretty boring, and I only got a small amount.

My stomach gurgled and hurt, wanting more food. I tried to tell myself I would lose weight, and then adults would stop annoyingly pinching my plump cheeks. *Why, aren't you cute, Eva,* they'd say. *Or is it Miriam?* If the cheek pinching would stop, I told myself I could handle less food.

Then my stomach churned more and more, and all I wanted was to eat. If we were back home, we could have so many delicious things from our gardens and orchards. Losing weight was ridiculous. I couldn't believe I used to get envious of Aliz over her slim figure. I wanted to eat real meals again!

The people who lived near the ghetto must have known what was going on. Some of them ignored us. Others would sneak to the fence and toss food over. Even though it was just a little food, they were our heroes.

I kept looking to Mama and Papa about what to do,

and they had completely different reactions. Papa was determined to hold himself together and protect the family.

Mama, on the other hand, let herself fall apart. She looked at the barbed wire fortress, at our small amount of food, at Papa with his wounds, and she blamed herself.

"We should have gone to Palestine," she told Papa, weeping. She slept so little that there were dark circles under her eyes as if she were bruised.

I didn't know how to comfort my parents the way Mama knew how to comfort me. She was my angel from heaven. I remembered the embroidery in our kitchen: *Your mind is like a garden. Plant flowers so weeds can't grow.*

How could anyone have happy thoughts in a place like this? How could I help Mama feel better? And at the same time, I was uneasy. If Mama and Papa had listened to me earlier about moving, we wouldn't have been in this mess. It wasn't fair that grown-ups always thought they knew better than kids.

None of this shook Papa's faith. He continued to pray

feverishly, his burned hands around his prayer book. He seemed to be waiting for a miracle to help us.

I thought about things differently. I saw a world where the only laws were the ones the Nazis made. And those laws were created for one thing: to get the Nazis more and more power, while the rest of us could be cast aside like old trash. There was no justice here.

I heard other grown-ups exchanging rumors in the crowded, uncomfortable ghetto. Some words had to be whispered because they were so awful.

"They're killing Jews in Germany." Whisper, whisper.

"They will not send us there."

"They might send us there."

"We can't think that way. As long as we stay out of Germany, we have a chance."

CHAPTER SEVEN

In the Train

It might have been May. More than two weeks had passed, but no one trapped in the ghetto knew for sure how long it had been. Nazi guards went into each tent and talked to the people there. One guard came to our tent, holding his gun.

"It's time to leave," the guard said evenly. "Everything you need will be at the camp, so you don't need to pack. That will just make the train more crowded."

None of us liked the idea of leaving our things behind. Mama and my older sisters sneaked some food with us so that we would be better prepared. Papa had his prayer book. Miriam and I dressed in identical burgundy dresses.

As the Jewish families got ready, the Nazi guards told us more about what was going on. They promised we were going to a labor camp in Hungary. No one said anything about going to Germany, which made a lot of people feel better.

"This is for your own protection," one of the guards said. "If you work, you will live. Your families will stay together."

Even though the guards were acting very calm, their guns told us they could become violent in a moment. And I was wary about believing Nazis. They kept lying to us.

"Papa," I said, tugging on his sleeve. He looked down at me. I wanted so much for him to fight back, to protect us. He must have seen by now that sitting back and taking abuse only made things worse.

"Papa," I said. "We shouldn't do this. We should not go."

I held Miriam's hand like a security blanket. If she felt the same way I did, she didn't say so. It always came down to me being the noisy one.

"Hush, Eva," Papa said, his voice somewhere between comforting and trying to make me stop talking. "Just do as they say and you will be okay."

Okay in a labor camp? I wasn't so sure. Edit, Aliz, Miriam, and I couldn't work as hard as a grown-up could. Papa was still hobbling and Mama wasn't totally over being sick, so I didn't know how well they could work, either. Would the Nazis put up with that?

Thousands of tired, weakened Jews came out of their tents, and the Nazis directed all of us to train tracks. The trains waiting there were cattle cars used for moving animals. Since Nazis thought of Jews as animals, the train choice made sense to them. The train cars had only a few windows, and they were up very high and covered with more barbed wire.

The Nazis wanted to fit as many Jews on as possible, so they kept sending more in. Soon the train car I stood in had maybe one hundred people squashed together. Everyone had to stand.

It was so cramped that people leaned against one another in the car. There were no bathrooms, either. My family stuck very close together. Mama held Miriam's and my hands in each of hers, as if she'd never let go. Papa held his prayer book the same way.

A Nazi ordered Papa to be in charge of the cattle car we were in. I don't know why he chose Papa. But the Nazi made two things very clear: One, if anyone escaped from the car, the Nazis would consider it Papa's fault. And two, if someone did escape, the Nazis would shoot Papa. The look in the Nazi's eye and the way he held his gun told us this was not an idle threat.

The train door was loudly and fiercely shut. We listened as a bar was put over the door. That meant that the only way we might get out was through the windows. One look at the barbed wire on those windows told me we weren't going anywhere.

With the door shut, the car became very dark. Then the train began to move, speeding up. There was a nonstop clacking as the train roared over the tracks.

All of this made me feel very panicky. No one had told us how long we'd have to be trapped in here. But then the train kept going and going, and nothing else happened. The panicky feeling turned to numbness. My thoughts went nowhere. None of this could be real.

When Mama had packed our food, she hadn't gotten us any water. My mouth got drier and drier, and then that was all I could think about. Hours must have passed. Then the train mysteriously stopped. We could hear the Nazis refueling.

"May we please have some water?" Papa called out through the barbed wire. By then the whole train was probably as thirsty as me.

The Nazi guard called back to Papa, "Five gold watches for water!"

I thought that was really something. Gold watches were expensive. Imagine trading them for just a little water! But the Nazis had the upper hand here, and people began taking off their gold watches. In the dim light of the train car, gold glinted as it was removed. I was surprised anyone still had any gold after the Nazis had gone family by family, demanding riches. Papa passed the five gold watches through the window, desperate to help out.

In response, a Nazi heaved a big bucket of water at the window and poured it down. We were not prepared, and most of the water just fell on people or the floor. The Nazis must have thought this was very funny.

Then the train started up again and we continued, just as thirsty as before.

CHAPTER EIGHT

Where Are We Going?

Miriam swore we were on that train for a whole week. It wasn't really that long, but it felt as if it would never end. Without food or water, our stomachs rumbled and our mouths got cottony. I kept swallowing saliva to try to feel better.

The only good thing about not eating or drinking was that I didn't have to go to the bathroom. Figuring out how to handle that in the crowded train car would have made things even worse.

When we stopped to refuel the next day, Papa called out the window for more water. The Nazi had the same answer: "Five gold watches for a drink!"

There was a helpless feeling in the car. Five grown-ups removed their gold watches and passed them over. The Nazi threw in a bucket of water again. This time we were better prepared. Papa had a bucket by the window and caught as much as he could. Then the bucket was sent around the train so that everyone could have a little. I also had a little cup with me that Mama had packed. I put it over my head when the Nazi threw in the water, hoping I would catch a big splash. I only got a few drops. That was all anyone could get.

While we were traveling, someone died in the car. This terrified everyone. I was glad I couldn't see the body.

When the train stopped, Papa called out, "Guard! Guard!"

"What do you want, you dirty Jew?" came the guard's nasty answer.

"Someone has died in here," Papa said. "Can we remove the body?"

We could hear the guard's laughter, as if he thought this was hysterically funny. No one came to get the body. Maybe someone said the Kaddish, the Jewish prayer of mourning. But the train continued on, clicking along the tracks and sometimes blowing its horn.

I could only hold Mama's hand and look around me. I was especially stunned by how willing the grown-ups were to give up their gold watches. Then I wondered if maybe it wasn't just about the water. Maybe they were also trying to get along with the Nazis to learn where we were going.

When the train stopped on the third day, Papa called out for water. He was ready with his bucket.

A voice called back, *"Was? Was?"*

I recognized the word from Aliz and Edit's tutor. The person was asking in German, "What? What?"

We must've been in Germany! Or if not Germany, one of the countries that the Nazis had taken over.

I felt drenched in terror. Cries and wails came from the train as we realized what this meant. Even though I didn't trust the Nazis, I knew it was possible we really were going to a labor camp in Hungary. Now the rumors about killing Jews in Germany felt too real. Some people were so frozen with fear that they could only stand there, unable to move or speak. Others were crying out to God to save them. I had heard many prayers in my life, but none as desperate as these. Some adults muffled their tears so they wouldn't scare their kids.

The train started back up again, the wheels speeding rapidly. Wherever we were going, the Nazis wanted us there in a hurry.

The train stopped again around daybreak.

"Guard!" Papa called through the barbed wire. "Guard!" No answer.

I tried looking through the window to figure out where we were. All I could see was barbed wire. Barbed wire and a gray, overcast sky.

As small as the windows were, they were letting in some kind of terrible, sickly sweet smell. It reminded me of when Papa's fingers and toes had been burned. Only it was so many times worse. I didn't know what it was.

Grown-ups pushed up to the windows to peek out. Others asked what they could see. "It looks so desolate," one man said, peering out.

Desolate meant joyless and lifeless. Whatever was out there, I had a pretty good feeling this was where we had been heading the whole time.

CHAPTER NINE

Our Promise to Papa

The Nazis still didn't tell us what was going on. There was more praying and crying. Papa fussed over which direction was east because he needed to say his morning prayers facing Jerusalem. He opened his prayer book, still trying to be a good Jew. He couldn't sense the rage swelling in me.

It was as if all the anger I'd been holding in for years was rushing to the surface. Here we were, possibly about to die, and no one had ever listened to me. I was wrong for being a Jew, wrong for being a girl, wrong for wanting to leave our home, wrong for not wanting to get on the train. Wrong, wrong, wrong! I was tired of being told there was something wrong with me.

Seeing Papa pray so peacefully just sent me over the edge. He thought prayer was the best response to all this. I thought he was counting on miracles too much and not doing enough in the here and now!

"Papa, what are you doing?" I snapped.

"Eva, we must say our daily prayers," Papa said, his typical Papa answer.

"Prayers?" I scoffed. Here it was again: Papa and me arguing, not seeing eye to eye. In all those times he'd scolded me or put me in the cellar, he'd never listened to what I had to say. I didn't argue with him to be a brat. I argued with him when something didn't make sense to me.

But it wasn't just my anger at how Papa was acting. It was my anger from years of being called a dirty Jew. My anger at Mrs. Margit. My anger at the Nazis. I had no power to attack them. I could attack Papa. And I let him have it.

"Papa, we have arrived somewhere, and we don't even know where we are!" I exclaimed. "They have lied to us! We are not in a work camp! We have been shut up like cattle in this car, without food or water. And you want to pray?"

I expected him to get angry at me. But he only looked at me calmly. Sadly. And he said in a soft voice, "Eva, Eva. We must pray. We must pray to God for mercy."

"Here in this place, wherever it is, you are still praying!" I shot back. "What good is it doing?"

And still he didn't get mad at me. "Eva, come," he said. "God will hear our prayers." Somehow in that crowded car he drew Mama, my sisters, and me all together. It was as if everything else in the cattle car fell away. He held us close.

One by one, Papa looked directly into our eyes. "Promise me that if any of you survives this terrible war, you will go to Palestine, where your uncle Aaron lives and where Jews can live in peace."

He was not talking to me as if I were silly, spoiled Eva. Or naughty Eva or difficult Eva.

He spoke to us all as equals, as family.

I realized then that when Papa had come back from the Nazi questioning at the ghetto, he hadn't just been broken in body. His spirit had also realized the full power of the Nazis, and he knew that it would not be too much longer before the Nazis swallowed us whole, like the Big Bad Wolf. The scariest stories Mama had told me before bed were nothing compared with the scary reality that we were living in. Papa did not expect to survive the war. He just wanted to make sure we did.

We all swore that we would move to Palestine. I had no more heart to argue with Papa. He turned to what he believed was the east and began to pray.

CHAPTER TEN

Arrival at
Auschwitz

Our time together as a family was broken. Angry shouts blared from outside the train. All the words were in German. I could also hear dogs barking. These dogs sounded as vicious and angry as the Nazis.

"*Schnell! Schnell! Raus!*" the Nazis shouted. *Hurry! Hurry! Get out!*

Someone removed the bars over our doors. Then the doors were flung open. SS guards stood outside, pointing guns at us. SS stood for Schutzstaffel, and these were the Nazi special police. They were all dressed in uniform, and I could see a skull and two small cross-bones on their hats. The SS were holding big dogs that were straining on their leashes, growling and showing fangs. These were not adorable, sweet pet dogs—they were trained to attack.

The only thing scarier was what lay behind them.

There was more barbed wire, fence after fence of barbed wire, all surrounding brown wooden buildings that stood out against the overcast sky. Looming guard towers hung over the buildings, and in each I could see at least one Nazi with his gun pointed toward us. There were so many people around, but it felt so lifeless at the same time, as if no one dared to breathe there. People cried or screamed instead. The air was full of that terrible smell.

One look told me this place hadn't been thrown together quickly like the ghetto. It had taken a lot of planning to create this. I didn't know whether hell was real, but if it was, I knew this was what it would look like.

Everyone got off the trains. It was a blur. White-haired older people needed aid, and they were lifted down by younger, stronger passengers. Some of the little kids looked so glad to be out of the trains that they ran around, stretching their legs. They were still too young to feel the terror that I felt. Shawled women clutched their babies close, trying to protect them.

Mama held Miriam's and my hands just as firmly. I was scared that if I let go of Mama, I'd lose her in the crowd. At the same time, none of this felt real. If the train hadn't been real, this surely couldn't be. Anytime now I was going to open my eyes and realize it was all a dream. A nightmare.

Then I felt how much Miriam was trembling and that brought me back to the moment. I grabbed her hand, too. The three of us were like a circle, unable to let go.

The sounds of screams increased. So did the sounds of prayers.

The SS forced us to line up on a concrete ramp. No one knew what was going on except for the Nazis, who marched through and studied us, looking for something.

I turned to Papa, Edit, and Aliz. They were gone! Somehow between our being on the train and getting off, they'd been swallowed in the pushing, crying, frantic crowd. I strained my eyes, trying to find them. There were too many heads above me, too many bodies around me. I could barely see anything.

I didn't know it then, but we had arrived in Poland, a country that the Nazis had taken over. Where Nazi law was the only law.

And the Nazis had a new law. Behind closed doors, leaders of the Nazi Party had discussed what to do about what they called the Jewish Problem. The fact that even a single Jew lived on this planet was a problem to them. The Nazis had been trying to take us out one by one: by treating us like animals, by trying to make us leave, by killing us when they could, and by making us live in ghettos. It wasn't good enough.

The Nazi leadership was made up of the most powerful men in Europe at the time. Their talks are full of mystery, but in the end, they came up with something called the Final Solution to the Jewish Problem. They were going to round up every Jew within reach and send them to death camps, a kind of concentration camp. Labor camps were created to get people to work as slaves, and death camps were exactly what they sounded like. Anyone caught helping Jews would be punished severely. Besides Jews, the Nazis sent Romani, Poles, political prisoners, prisoners of war, and other groups to death camps, too.

None of us in the crowd knew all these details then. We only knew fear and confusion. There we were, standing at the entrance of Auschwitz, the Nazis' most notorious death camp.

"*Schnell! Schnell!*" the Nazis yelled, driving us like cattle.

At the same time, I heard one SS guard calling out a different word over and over. "*Zwillinge! Zwillinge!*" he shouted, running through the crowds. That was another German word I knew. It meant, *Twins! Twins!*

He went right past Miriam, Mama, and me, realized something, and turned back around. He looked me up and down, then looked Miriam up and down. We were wearing the exact same burgundy dresses. Then he looked back and forth from one of us to the other.

Go away, go away! I wanted to tell him. *Leave my family and me alone!*

"Are they twins?" he asked Mama in German as I shivered under his cold eyes.

Twins? Why does it matter? What could this Nazi possibly want with Miriam and me?

CHAPTER ELEVEN

Separated from Mama

Mama also spoke some German, but she hesitated, not knowing why a Nazi would care that we were twins. Finally, she asked in German, "Is that a good thing?"

"Yes," the SS guard told her.

"They are twins," Mama admitted.

The SS guard snatched Miriam and me by the arms, ripping us out of Mama's hands. "No!" I screamed, trying to fight him. "Mama, Mama!"

My hands waved out wildly, trying to hold Mama again. No matter how much I dug my heels in or begged him, the guard didn't stop racing away with us.

"Eva! Miriam!" Mama wailed. She tried to come after us, her arms outstretched to gather us back to her. Another Nazi guard seized her and pulled her into the crowd. I couldn't see her anymore!

"*Mama!*" I shrieked. The guard forced Miriam and me with him past the railroad tracks. At the platform, the Jews were being divided into two sections. Stronger young men and women were on one side. Children, old people, and sickly-looking people were on the other. My family wasn't the only one being torn apart.

"Mama!" I cried. Tears blinded me. In my head, all I could see was Mama's face before we lost sight of her.

Suddenly, the SS guard halted. We were surrounded by other twins who had been found in the trains. Some of the twins were very little, and some were teenagers. In my shock, my tears dried up. What was going on here?

Then I was in for another shock. A woman and her twin children joined us, prodded on by a different

SS guard. The woman was Mrs. Csengeri, a friend of Mama's!

Mrs. Csengeri lived close to our village, and she and Mama would chat about how to take care of twins. Mrs. Csengeri's twin daughters, Yehudit and Lea, were close to Miriam's and my age, so we would play games while our mamas caught up.

Miriam and I quickly got up close to Mrs. Csengeri. Her daughters were so lucky. They got to have their mama around when we didn't! I just couldn't get over how strange all this was. I didn't see any other types of people being separated like we were. Everyone else had been put into one of those two lines on the platform.

True, I knew that many people found twins fascinating, especially identical ones like Miriam and me. But I didn't see why the Nazis cared whether someone was a twin or not. Or why they thought it was a good thing.

Half an hour later, after the twins were collected, the Nazis took us into a building that had bleachers on one side, like at a gymnasium or sports arena. The other side was set up with showers. Besides the Nazis, there were a few fragile-looking women in there wearing striped blue-and-white outfits.

"Undress!" an SS guard barked out.

I didn't undress in front of strangers. I certainly didn't undress in front of Nazis! That was much too embarrassing.

Miriam started to undress. I found myself doing the same. I kept having the feeling that this wasn't real. This wasn't me taking off my burgundy dress. This wasn't me standing naked in front of all these armed Nazi men.

Next our hair was cut. Why did we need to take our clothes off for that? A woman wearing a striped outfit snipped her scissors all around my head, talking to me.

"You twins are very privileged," the barber said in German. "You receive special treatment."

I understood enough German to get the idea that normally prisoners here weren't allowed to keep any hair. The woman almost made it sound as if I should be thankful that I was being treated better.

I was numb. My hair fell to the ground and was no longer a part of me.

They cut Miriam's hair, too. Now our hair only went

to just below our ears. Mrs. Csengeri's hair was shaved completely off.

We were sent into the showering area to get clean. After that we got our clothes back. What a relief! I saw that someone had painted a red cross on our dresses, though. It made me think of how the Nazis made us wear yellow stars. This red cross on our clothes symbolized something.

What?

My anger spiked up. This dress might be the last thing I had from Mama, and they had ruined it. I was tired of obeying. Whatever they wanted to do to me next, I wouldn't let them.

I felt that way even more strongly when I saw what came next. The Nazis were having another woman in a striped outfit tattoo everyone's arm, one at a time. Each new person was told to hold out an arm. Then their arm was held down by Nazis, and the woman with the tattooing needle set to work. I could see the pain in people's faces as ink pricked into their skin.

I wouldn't give them my arm. Never! When they came at me, I kicked and fought with everything I had in me. An SS guard brutally seized my left arm. The feel of his grip digging into my flesh sent me off into a new level of fury. Papa wasn't around to tell me to behave. The Nazis treated us horribly no matter what we did, even when we obeyed their every word.

Well, I would give those Nazis trouble. "I want my mama!" I shrieked.

"Hold still!" the SS guard commanded.

I saw the tattoo needle being heated over a long flame in a lamp. I couldn't get loose. So I did the only thing I could think of. I opened my mouth and sank my teeth into the arm of the Nazi holding me, biting him as hard as I could.

CHAPTER TWELVE

A-7063 and A-7064

Three other Nazis rushed over to hold me down.

As soon as I stopped biting, I screamed, "Bring back my mama!"

"We will let you see her tomorrow," one of the Nazis said.

Lies! I kept struggling. Miriam watched everything, shocked. With four Nazi guards holding me down, I really had no chance of getting away now. The tattooing needle was dipped in ink and set against my arm.

Even though I knew it was going to hurt, I hadn't expected this much pain.

"Stop!" I cried. The Nazis held me even more tightly. Numbers slowly appeared across my skin. Every single line was created by a series of stabbing dots. "That hurts!"

The numbers came out small and shaky, thanks to all my fighting. Still, the Nazis had won this battle. I had been branded by them.

They released me and I looked down at my sore, swollen skin. It wouldn't stop aching and burning. Then it was Miriam's turn to get tattooed. She took the pain without a word, and definitely without biting anyone. When they were done, the number on her arm was easy to read.

I was A-7063 and she was A-7064. Like prisoners in jail, we had been given numbers so the Nazis could keep track of us. To them, we weren't Eva and Miriam Mozes anymore. We were children who had no names.

Once everyone had been tattooed, the Nazis said it

was time to move again. We were under tight guard as we walked through Auschwitz. Violent prisoners might get the same sort of treatment.

Walking through Auschwitz let me get a good look at the place. I still didn't see Mama, Papa, Edit, or Aliz anywhere. I did see lots more Nazis, and some of them were holding more of those vicious-looking big dogs. I also saw people who were so thin they looked like skeletons. I'd had no idea that people could get so thin and still be alive. They were wearing the same striped outfits as the barber and the tattooist. These were other prisoners. Other Jews. And even they were surrounded by Nazi guards, as if they were violent criminals. They looked too weak to harm a fly.

One of the skinny prisoners saw us walking by. Her eyes widened. She stepped out of line and walked toward us as if nothing else existed.

"Children," the poor skinny woman said. Her haunted eyes almost seemed to glow when they looked at us. "Who are you? I need to find my children. Do you know what happened to my children?"

The Nazis were furious that she'd stepped out of line

to talk to us. Two of the Nazi guards dropped the leashes and let their dogs free.

"Attack!" a Nazi commanded. The dogs attacked the woman.

We were forced to keep marching, as if none of that had happened.

Our new home—the barracks, the Nazis called it—was one of the big wooden buildings. When I looked inside, it reminded me of a barn. I wasn't silly for thinking that. Later I learned that people used to keep horses there. Two long windows ran along the top of the barracks.

Bunk beds, each with three beds, lined the walls. One brick bench split the room in half, and one small oven stood at each end.

Many identical faces looked back at us from the bunks. This was where all the twin Jewish girls were kept. The twin Jewish boys had a different building.

All the girls had their own set of numbers tattooed on their arms. Even the toddlers.

On the far end was a little room called a latrine for

when we needed to use the bathroom. It was just three holes in the cement floor. Whatever went down into that latrine stayed there.

We were told, again, how lucky we twins were. Most prisoners did not have their own latrine.

Right after we arrived, dinner was announced. The kids who'd already been there hurried to one end of the barracks, eager. It had been days since I'd eaten, and I was shaky and full of nervous energy.

When I saw what was being served to us, I couldn't understand why the other kids were so excited. It was only bread and some kind of brown liquid in a cup. Some of the other twins explained that the brown liquid was "fake coffee." I had no idea what was in it.

The bread was thick. Two and a half inches. And very dark. It didn't look tasty at all.

I told one of the Hungarian twins what my sister and I were both thinking. "We can't eat this," I said.

"It's all you will get until tomorrow," the Hungarian twin said, ripping into her bread as if it were a delicious meal. "You had better eat it."

"It's not kosher," I said. I didn't think God would

like me eating nonkosher food. Worse, what would Papa think?

The twins burst out laughing, as if I'd said something very funny.

"Here, you can have it," I said, offering my bread. Following my lead, Miriam handed her bread to the other twins.

The twins didn't say "Are you sure?" Or "No, you should have it." They gobbled the bread down until there weren't even crumbs left. And they drank that disgusting-looking fake coffee.

One of the older twins watched this and thought she could share some wisdom. "We are glad to have the extra portion," she told Miriam and me. "But the two of you are going to have to learn to eat everything if you want to survive. You cannot be fussy. And you cannot worry about whether or not something is kosher."

"We cannot violate God's law," I said, echoing Papa's words.

The older twin shook her head. Her eyes shared more wisdom with me: *There are no laws here.*

CHAPTER THIRTEEN

Fire and Smoke

Seeing how innocent Miriam and I were, some of the other twins decided they needed to educate us. They began by telling us where we were. "You are in Birkenau," one twin said. "It is part of Auschwitz. But it is three kilometers from the main camp."

That meant it was a little less than two miles. Simple enough. But when the twins started talking about gas chambers and crematoriums, we were lost.

"What is a gas chamber?" I asked. "What is a crematorium?" I'd never heard of either of those things before.

"Follow us, and we'll show you," one twin said. We went to the end of the barracks, and the twins pointed to the sky. When I'd seen the sky earlier, it had simply looked overcast. Gray. Depressing. Now I saw chimneys rising above the buildings of Auschwitz. Piping-hot flames writhed out of each chimney, turning the sky around it a sinister red. The flames pumped out enough smoke to cover the whole camp. And there was ash, so much ash. It was falling down like millions of tears.

The awful smell I'd noticed earlier was stronger than ever.

Despite the heat of the flames, I felt myself go cold in my whole body. "What are they burning so late in the evening?" I made myself ask.

"People," a twin said.

"You don't burn people!" I exclaimed, turning on her. "Don't be ridiculous!"

"The Nazis do," another twin said. "They want to kill all the Jews."

I shook my head. "Nobody can kill all the Jews," I argued.

"The Germans are trying." The twins all sounded so knowledgeable. They all sounded so matter-of-fact about the most awful things. "After every transport arrives, the chimneys glow day and night."

When they said *transport*, I realized they meant *trains*. Like the train we had come in earlier.

"Did you see how the Nazis divided the people arriving on the trains into two groups this morning?" a twin asked.

Young men and women on one side. Children and old people on the other. Yes, I had seen.

This, the twin said, was the *selection process*.

"They are probably burning them right now," the twin continued. "Only those who can work will stay alive and only as long as they are strong enough to work. The weak, the sick, the old, and the young end up in the flames."

My thoughts flew to still-fragile Mama. And to hobbling Papa. To my older sisters, barely teenagers.

Then to the other people on the train. The old

people who could scarcely walk. The kids who'd liked stretching their legs when we got off. The newborn babies being held tightly in their mamas' arms.

Part of me sank down with the horror that these twins were telling the truth. The chimneys were too convincing. The ashes falling might be the ashes of my family.

And another part screamed at those thoughts and wouldn't believe them. Papa was hobbling, but he was still strong. Edit and Aliz weren't small children, so they could work. And Mama...

"They are burning people," another twin said, seeing the look on my face. "Don't you know that they are killing everybody that is here?"

"We are children," I argued. "We can't work, but we're still alive."

"For now," another twin said. So calmly. So used to this.

"Only those who can work or who have some use are left alive," a different twin added.

Some use?

I still wouldn't accept this. "So why are we so privileged?"

"We might be killed someday, but right now they want us alive because we are twins," a twin said.

"We are used for experiments," another explained. "Dr. Mengele does them."

Who?

"Dr. Mengele will be here tomorrow, right after roll call," a twin said. "You will find out tomorrow why you were not taken to the gas chamber immediately."

They were saying the name Dr. Mengele as if he were a god, or a demon. Or both. "Wh-what experiments are you talking about?" I stammered.

A twelve-year-old Hungarian twin swooped in. "Eva and Miriam," she said, because we weren't just numbers to her. She was trying to be comforting, like Mama. "I really want you to stop worrying about it. It's not so bad. I think you'd better go to bed now. It's been a difficult day for you."

CHAPTER FOURTEEN

My Vow

Kids crawled into bunk beds, still wearing their clothes. No one had pajamas. Miriam and I lay down at the bottom of one of the bunks. There was straw underneath us.

I felt exhausted but unable to sleep. I couldn't stop seeing the chimneys in my mind and thinking about what the other twins had said.

Movement on the floor caught my attention.

I looked more closely. Something else moved. Then

I realized what I must be seeing. "There are mice in here!" I shrieked.

No one else jumped up in panic.

"Quiet," shushed an annoyed twin, trying to sleep. "Those are not mice. They are rats, and they will not hurt you if you don't have any food in your bed. Go back to sleep."

The other twins rolled over and slept. I couldn't. I watched as more movement shimmered along the floor. These were the biggest rats I had ever seen. They were the same size as little cats. I could imagine their teeth cutting into me like tattoo needles.

I snuggled in closer to Miriam. She couldn't sleep, either. For a long time we lay there. Then I began to feel some discomfort below my stomach. For the first time in days I needed to use the bathroom. I asked Miriam and she needed to use it, too.

Holding hands, we climbed out of the bunk bed and headed for the latrine. Rats scampered out of our way.

I knew we were getting closer to the latrine because of the smell. When I'd seen the latrine earlier, I'd realized that not everyone had been able to make it to the holes in time. It was not going to be a pretty sight.

Even knowing this did not prepare me. When we stepped into the little room, Miriam and I both pulled back, horrified.

Three naked children lay on the floor there, perfectly still. They were as thin as skeletons, and their eyes were fixed on the ceiling, not moving.

They were dead.

My knees almost buckled under me. This was the first time I'd ever seen a dead body, let alone three. For the first time, the feeling of unreality left me. I could not deny the smoking chimneys or the terrifying stories anymore. I really had seen two lines of people earlier, one that was being sent to immediate death, one that was being sent to work until they died.

I also had tried to block from my mind the scene earlier with the woman and the dogs, and now I couldn't. Those dogs hadn't just jumped on that woman. They had killed her before my very eyes.

Everything the twins had told me was true. The Nazis did want to kill every single Jew. When Jews and other unwanted people first arrived at death camps like Auschwitz, there was a "selection," which Miriam, the other twins, and I had survived because we were twins. Nazi doctors were in charge of the selection, picking which people looked healthy enough to work and which ones weren't worth the Nazis' time. The living, breathing people viewed as not worth their time were sent to the gas chambers. The Nazis tricked them into believing they were going to take a shower. Then the people were locked into the building and a poisonous gas called Zyklon B was lowered into the vents. People forced into a small area with it couldn't breathe. It was an easy way for the Nazis to kill whole groups of people at a time.

Later I learned that the Nazis sent 90 percent of Jews arriving at Auschwitz straight to the gas chambers. Anyone under fifteen years old was sent. Anyone too old or too weak to work was sent. Then the bodies were usually thrown into giant ovens, called crematoriums. The bodies were turned to ashes and sent out into the sky.

There have been many times in history when one group has turned on another and tried to kill everyone in that second group. It's now called genocide. But this was the first time that genocide had been so carefully plotted and so massively enforced. It was also the first time people had the kind of technology for such a large-scale killing. Before the war was over, Nazis and their helpers would murder two out of every three Jews in Europe.

Even though I didn't know all those details then, an overwhelming feeling of loss and horror swept over me.

But I felt something else. I felt the Eva in me who fought back, who argued against authority, who wouldn't sit back and take things the way they were. It was time to take charge.

I will survive, I vowed. *And Miriam will survive.*

We were not going to end up on the floor like these children. We were not going to be killed in the gas chambers. No matter what it took, we were going to walk out of the gates of Auschwitz at the end of the war. Alive.

I did not tell my vow to Miriam. She was crying. If I told her, she might say, *But how, Eva, how?*

That would put doubt in my mind. There were two things a person needed to survive in Auschwitz: an unending desire for survival, and luck. I didn't have any control over my luck, but I would not give up an ounce of my desire for survival.

I will protect you, Miriam, I thought. *We will make it through this.*

My hand sought out Miriam's hand. We were two girls against the Nazi regime. We returned to bed and huddled together, my vow coursing through my veins.

CHAPTER FIFTEEN

Dr. Mengele Arrives

"Dr. Mengele is coming!" a female SS guard shouted the next morning.

We'd been woken up while it was still dark and were made to go outside and be counted in roll call. The dead children I'd seen had died in their beds, and the other kids had moved them to the latrine. Because who wanted to sleep next to the bodies? The still-alive kids took their clothing since dead kids had no need for it but we did.

I was in for a new surprise after roll call when we returned to the barracks. The SS had taken the dead children and put them back in their bunks, as if they were sleeping. Anyone who even glanced over would know that wasn't true.

And now the SS guard was yelling about this Dr. Mengele. The twins all lined up against the bunks, backs straight, hands held behind them. This pose made them look like little soldiers waiting for orders from their commanding officer. Miriam and I copied what they were doing.

The kids' actions weren't the strangest thing, though. The Nazi guards were trembling. I didn't know Nazis could feel fear. Whoever this Dr. Mengele was, he made even the people on his own side quake at the thought of him.

Footsteps.

All our eyes were on the door, waiting. It felt as if the whole room had stopped breathing.

And then a dark-haired man in a white lab coat strode into the barracks. He held himself as if the whole room and everyone in it belonged to him and he knew it. And enjoyed it. A trail of doctors and assistants came in behind him, watching his every move in worshipful silence.

Still, I sensed fear in them.

He must have been in his early thirties. Below his white lab coat I could see his dark pant legs and his knee-high black boots. Little high heels on those shiny black boots made smart clacks across the floor. The collar of his Nazi uniform peeked out from above the lab coat, showing the symbols of the SS. On his head was the SS hat—a skull and crossbones blazing.

He swirled a baton around in his gloved hands. All his movements were graceful, the sound of his boots elegant. The word for him was *aristocratic*. This man had never known the struggles of a peasant. He looked like someone who'd spent his whole life being applauded by friends and family for how great he was, and now he believed every word of it.

This was Dr. Mengele.

Even though doctors are supposed to heal and help, he didn't look at all worried to see so many abused, starving children. He moved from bunk to bunk, very calm and composed, taking roll call like a teacher.

It wasn't until he reached the dead children that he changed. The baton stopped swirling in his hands.

He turned on the SS guards, savagely angry.

"Why did these children die?" he thundered. The guards cowered in fear and tried to come up with excuses. Dr. Mengele would have none of it.

"I cannot afford to even lose one child!" the doctor roared. His face twisted up in all the ugliness anger can create. I didn't remember ever seeing a grown-up that angry before. I wanted to crawl under the straw and hide.

There was more apologizing from the SS guards. Dr. Mengele stood there fuming. Then he stalked on, continuing down the row. The clacks of his boots had gone from elegant to the sound of thunder.

Don't look at me, I pleaded silently, as if he could hear me. *Ignore us. You don't want Miriam and me.*

Dr. Mengele's boots stopped directly in front of me. My head came up to just above his waist. Our eyes locked. He had a stethoscope tucked into one of his lab coat pockets, but even without it he could probably hear how loudly my heart was pounding.

His eyes turned to Miriam, coldly studying her.

Then without a word Dr. Mengele continued on. His trail of doctors followed.

After Dr. Mengele left, we were given breakfast. It was the same fake coffee as the night before. There was no bread. My poor stomach hurt. Miriam and I drank the coffee, hoping for some strength.

I could not get that first meeting with Dr. Mengele out of my mind. He'd been so furious about the dead children. Did that mean he cared about us? If he cared about us, you'd think we'd be treated better.

I tried getting more information out of the other twins. They kept saying the same things: Dr. Mengele was obsessed with twins. He wanted to use us for medical experiments. No, they didn't know what those experiments were.

He'd also saved our lives. So far. Since we were

under fifteen, we would have been sent right to the gas chambers if we hadn't been twins.

"Do you remember the selection process we told you about?" one twin asked. I nodded.

"Dr. Mengele does those."

It turned out Dr. Mengele was not the only doctor who did selections at Auschwitz. There were a few others. But everyone thought of Dr. Mengele as the doctor who did the selections. The one who chose who would live and who would die.

Some of the other Nazi doctors had trouble with the selection process. It was easy to hate Jews because of all the anti-Jewish stories they'd been fed by the Nazis. It was another thing to look actual Jewish men, women, and children in the eyes and decide whether they would live or not. Some of these doctors had to get stinking drunk before selections or they felt too guilty.

Not Dr. Mengele, I was told.

Dr. Mengele never needed a drink to dull his senses. The selection process was exactly why I hadn't seen him the day before. While I was taken off with the other twins, Dr. Mengele was behind those crowds of people from the trains. He separated them into the two lines. He used the baton to point left or right. Sometimes he whistled music like *The Blue Danube* waltz while he did it.

We twins were his property now, so he could do whatever he wanted with us. He hadn't gotten angry because he cared about those dead children. He was furious because they'd died too soon and ruined his experiment.

The supervisors called for us to get ready. It was time for the day's experiments to begin.

CHAPTER SIXTEEN

Experiments

The SS divided us into groups of five and marched us across Auschwitz to a large two-story brick building. Lots of boy twins were already there. Somehow the twin boys had a Jewish man named Zvi Spiegel watching over them. Zvi tried to take good care of his boys, getting them a soccer ball made of rags to play with and making sure they learned one another's names so they still felt human. The boys loved him and called him the Twins' Father.

We girl twins didn't have anyone like him, and I didn't know a lot of the other twin girls' names. We each felt alone, thinking about our survival more than anything else. What a difference having someone like Zvi would have made for us!

I quickly spotted Dr. Mengele in the building. He had recovered from the temper tantrum he'd thrown earlier and was all business, ready to work.

We were told we had to take our clothes off.

It was like the showers all over again! I don't think a single one of the twins wanted to obey. But every single one of us did. The Nazis had us sit on benches. Some of the girls were so embarrassed to be naked in front of these Nazi men. They tried covering themselves with their hands. That made the Nazis laugh and point.

Dr. Mengele did not laugh and point. He acted above all that. It was very cold in the room.

While Dr. Mengele watched and gave directions, the other Nazi doctors began their experiments. The

Nazi doctors were all men, and they were all dressed like Dr. Mengele, with white lab coats over their Nazi uniforms.

There were also Jewish prisoners working there, both men and women. When the trains came into Auschwitz, the Nazis would look for people with medical training. These doctors had an uncomfortable choice: work for the Nazis or die. So here they were working, their heads down.

The day began with the doctors measuring the size of Miriam's head and mine. One doctor would measure and tell his results to an assistant. The assistant feverishly wrote everything down. They spent hours just studying the tiny differences between Miriam's and my ears.

They were especially interested in our eyes. Miriam and I both had big blue eyes. The Nazis wanted something they called racial purity, and their idea of this was to have all people be blond and blue-eyed. They thought it was Germanic looking, or Aryan as they called it. They thought of Jews as having dark skin and hair, though that isn't true. And not all Nazis were blond and blue-eyed. Hitler sure wasn't, with his black hair. Neither was Dr. Mengele. He had dark brown hair and hazel eyes.

The doctors looked at Miriam's and my eyes as if they had some sort of secret in them.

The Nazis had a chart of all different shades of blue eyes.

A photographer also took pictures of us, and an artist drew what we looked like. Sometimes a doctor would go and whisper with Dr. Mengele. When Dr. Mengele talked, I saw he had a gap between his top front teeth. I could never hear what the doctors said.

The Nazis also wanted to ask Miriam and me questions about ourselves, like our age and other personal information. This went on for maybe eight hours. Then we were sent back to the barracks, where we got fake coffee and a thick slice of bread. Miriam and I wolfed the bread down and drank the nasty-tasting coffee, not caring if it was kosher. Someone had removed the dead children's bodies from the barracks.

The next day, the Nazis wanted our blood.

We were taken to blood labs in Birkenau. I was so glad when they didn't make us take our clothes off. I'd never gotten a shot before or had any blood taken. Neither had Miriam.

They used one arm for taking blood and the other arm for giving shots. They kept writing everything down.

Of course, they didn't tell us what was in the shots or what the blood work was for. We just had to obey. And stay silent, unless asked to talk.

Miriam and I barely said anything to each other about these experiments. When they were going on, I tried to send my mind as far away as possible. *This isn't real. This can't be happening.* When we went back to the barracks at night, we didn't want to remember our day.

I got sent back to the tattooing station twice more because of how sloppy my number was.

They didn't know me very well if they thought *that* was going to work. I didn't bite, but I still wiggled and fought with all my might. I would show them. The Nazis could never get a decent set of numbers on my arm. Finally, they gave up. It was a small victory.

The days in Dr. Mengele's lab experiments turned into weeks, then months. Day after day we had to strip in front of Dr. Mengele and the Nazi doctors and be examined. Or we got to keep our clothes on and they pricked us with needles. Sometimes they tied us down so that we couldn't struggle. The doctors' hands roamed all over our bodies like spiders, burrowing in places they didn't belong.

Other kids had to go through much more terrible ordeals. There were children who lost their voices to Dr. Mengele's experiments on them. Now they could not tell their story, or even scream. He crippled other children so they couldn't walk. He tried turning boys into girls and girls into boys, and those experiments ended badly.

Sometimes one twin would mysteriously disappear, and we'd be informed they were "ill." Then the second twin would disappear, and neither one ever returned. I feared the worst. I now knew people were thrown into the gas chambers all the time at Auschwitz. They might be killed in other ways, too. Surviving the selection at arrival did not save you from being "selected" for death sometime later.

I felt like the children who'd had their voices stolen because I couldn't even cry for help.

At night we slept on straw that was squirming with lice. We could hear rats running around the barracks. Pretty soon Miriam and I both had lice itching and tormenting us. The barber shaved the little hair we had left, and that still didn't make the lice go away.

Miriam and I had to start picking lice off each other.

Seeing the lice infestation, Dr. Mengele ordered our barracks to be cleaned. It was only cleaned a little. The lice stayed like happy boarders.

As filthy as Auschwitz was, I never saw Dr. Mengele look less than dashing in his clean uniform and lab coat. The Nazis put signs all over the camp for themselves, like YOUR HEALTH DEPENDS ON CLEANLINESS.

Did a man trained in the art of healing see anything wrong with all the killing around him?

No, of course not. Because, to Nazis, Jews were animals. Worse. Termites, parasites. Creatures to be exterminated. The best way to turn someone into your enemy is to believe they're not human. To believe that they don't have hopes and fears and dreams like everyone else.

Sending Jews to the gas chambers, experimenting on them, all made sense to Dr. Mengele. Because who cared about a bunch of animals?

It seemed that no matter where we went, Dr. Mengele was there. Controlling us like puppets. Deciding our lives and deaths. Breathing down our necks. Watching with the cruelest of smiles on his face. Oh, how he loved his power.

CHAPTER SEVENTEEN

The Measure of a Man

"Dr. Mengele is so gorgeous," gushed one of the teenage girls above my bunk.

"He could be a movie star," agreed her twin sister, sighing romantically.

I couldn't believe my ears! Were they talking about the same man?

I think most of us twins were just plain scared of Dr. Mengele. I sure was.

But some of the teenage girls got mad crushes on him. They giggled and whispered about his smooth skin and perfect hair. They acted as if one day he might change his ways, sweep the girl into his arms, and take her away to Happily Ever After.

Some of the younger twins liked him, too. They saw him as their new papa. It really sickened me when he would gather the twins around him, smile angelically, and call us "meine Kinder." That was German for "my children."

I was not his child!

I heard stories that Dr. Mengele would bring in little sweets or treats for some of the twins. They loved him for that. He never gave me any. But I also heard stories that Dr. Mengele would give a twin some sweets one day, then kill them the very next. The sweets were like a last meal.

But how he loved twins! Later, I finally got an idea why. In science experiments, you have something called a control. It's something that's allowed to stay in its natural state so you can compare it to something you experiment on.

Let's say you want to see what will happen if you stop watering plants. You keep watering one plant so that it's the same as always. That's the control. But you can experiment on the other plant, which has to be the exact same kind of plant. Then you compare the control to the plant that isn't getting any water. If the control lives and the other plant wilts from no water, science has shown you that plants need water.

With twins, Dr. Mengele had the perfect control. We identical twins are nearly exactly alike in our looks and our DNA. So he could put diseases or chemicals in one twin and watch what happened. And he had the other twin to compare the results to.

With twins he thought he might be able to figure out how to create the perfect Aryan race and make Hitler proud. He was also obsessed with people with dwarfism, or anyone whose body was different from the way bodies were most of the time. Our bodies kept getting thinner and thinner without food until we looked like skeletons. Did watching starvation obsess him, too?

I think some of the other twins got crushes on him or thought of him as a father figure because it was the only way they could cope with the world they'd been thrown into. It might have felt safer to love Dr. Mengele instead of hate him.

They'd think, Dr. Mengele saved me from the gas chambers. He sneaks me treats. He doesn't hurt me, no, no. I owe everything to Dr. Mengele.

They'd think, My new papa, Dr. Mengele.

Or they'd think, My make-believe boyfriend, Dr. Mengele.

Dr. Mengele thought of himself as such a hotshot that he probably just soaked all this up. No one mentioned his wife or the baby son he left at home. And no one mentioned that we didn't have our papas because Dr. Mengele was probably the one who'd sent them to their deaths.

Yet the Nazis kept telling us we were privileged.

After a while I understood what they were trying to say. My first day at Auschwitz was a perfect example. There was a reason why a woman had been killed for just stepping out of line but I got away with biting a Nazi.

If the Nazi guard had killed me that day for biting

him, he'd have had to deal with Dr. Mengele's wrath. No one wanted that. Not even the Nazis.

On the one hand, Dr. Mengele was the only person keeping us alive. On the other hand, he was the only person allowed to kill us.

Meine Kinder, he whispered in my nightmares. Was I awake or was I asleep? Even though he never touched me and always had the other doctors do it, I felt as if his hands were all over me. Stealing who I was. Making me his. *There is no escaping.*

Meine Kinder.

CHAPTER EIGHTEEN

Day by Day

When the experiments weren't going on, Miriam and I helped care for the really little twins in the barracks. It gave us something normal feeling to do.

We ripped barbed wire from a fence surrounding a little yard near us and turned it into knitting needles. We weren't trying to make anything fancy. We just liked having something to do with our hands.

Mostly I did not think about my family anymore. I

blocked it out because...because, why? It was too painful to think about, and all my thoughts had to be on staying alive and protecting Miriam.

As much as we tried not to think about it, deep down we were all desperate to know what had happened to our families. So one day when we were out in the sunlight trying to knit, a prisoner pushing a cart nearby caught our attention. The cart was filled with dead bodies.

A fence blocked us from getting closer. We crowded at the fence, trying to see if there was anyone we knew in the cart.

"Mama!" a little girl next to me cried. Her eyes flooded with hot, wet tears. "It's my mama!"

I did not know which person in the pile was her mama. It was hard to even believe those bodies had once breathed, lived, held another, loved.

The little girl wept hysterically. She could not even get through the fence to wish her mama goodbye.

The prisoner kept pushing the cart, as if this was nothing new. So many prisoners in Auschwitz were forced to do the worst jobs because the Nazis couldn't be bothered.

A part of me wanted to comfort the girl. I did not know how. I could not tell her, *There, there, it will all be okay.* Because that was a lie.

Papa would declare that the Kaddish, the Jewish prayer of mourning, must be said for those who died. Every single day in Auschwitz was a long, silent Kaddish said by all those still living.

I did not see my mama in that cart. Still, I wondered whether she'd been in another cart on another day, and I'd missed seeing her.

I looked down at my dress. It was the last thing I had from Mama, and it was falling apart. I guessed that's what happened when you wore the same clothes day after day, night after night. Miriam's dress looked the same way.

The Nazis decided to give Miriam and me new clothes. Unlike Mama's perfectly tailored dresses, they handed us way-too-big women's dresses. This gave us something else to do. We got string and tied it around our waists to keep the dresses up.

The lice continued to infest us, even if we didn't

have hair and we kept up on our weekly showers. I was itchy all the time, my head scratched raw.

This was my life now. It was far away from home, far away from school, far away from any kind of childhood. I didn't feel like a kid anymore. I was always exhausted and on the watch for danger. And I was always hungry. The fake coffee never really helped my stomach, and we got bread only at night. That caused a problem. I wanted to save the bread till morning so that I could have it for breakfast. It gave me extra strength during the day that the coffee by itself didn't give.

But keeping the bread safe till morning was a challenge. The rats might try to steal it during the night. Or they might bite me. I spent a lot of time thinking about the best ways to eat my little bit of bread. I did not cry or feel sorry for myself over all this. I had become so numb that even the worst things I saw began to just feel normal.

We still saw Mama's friend Mrs. Csengeri sometimes. She lived with other women during the day, and at night she'd slip into the twins' barracks whenever she could.

Sometimes she sneaked extra food and clothes from the Nazis to give to her girls. The Nazis didn't notice her taking things, but sometimes they noticed her creeping into our barracks. If she got caught, she was beaten over the head by the guards.

Beating or no beating, it didn't stop her from visiting. I tried not to be gnawed open with envy when I'd see her hugging and kissing her daughters. Or when she'd give them little gifts like extra bread or a warm hat. I just stuck close to Miriam because if I had to take care of the two of us until we found Mama, then that was what I'd do. I just kept repeating my vow, giving myself strength.

And I would need that strength when I learned the terrible plans Dr. Mengele had in mind for Miriam and me.

CHAPTER NINETEEN

Sick!

Something was very wrong.

I had spent that summer day in the lab with the Nazi doctors drawing blood from one arm and giving me a shot in the other. I knew Dr. Mengele had ordered whatever shot they'd given me. But instead of going to the barracks to spend a usual evening, I began to feel bad. Then worse.

My body took turns being wracked with fire and

shuddering with chills. Each beat of my heart hammered in my head, hurting me. I lay next to Miriam in the barracks that night, exhausted but too achy to sleep. I could hear the sounds of rats scampering and people crying in the darkness. I couldn't take it anymore. I reached out and gently shook Miriam. She raised her head and looked at me sleepily.

"I'm v-v-very s-s-sick." My teeth chattered so hard I could barely talk.

Miriam went from sleepy to concerned. "What shall we do?"

Sick or not, she still saw me as the leader. "I d-d-don't know," I admitted. It was so hard to think. Everything was fuzzy. "L-l-let's try to hide it and pretend I'm all right."

The next day was Sunday, the one day the Nazis didn't experiment on us. I rested and rested. It didn't help my fever at all. Monday morning came, and I felt as bad as ever.

The supervisor yelled for us to get outside for roll call.

My legs wanted to give out from under me and my

head felt as if it had water sloshing around in it. I did not remember ever feeling this sick in my life. I hoped I didn't pass out.

Slowly, I stumbled outside.

If the supervisor didn't see my dizziness or chattering teeth, there was no way she'd miss all the red dots that had appeared on my legs. My arms and legs had gotten so swollen they had doubled in size. What should I do?

To survive Auschwitz, you needed a strong desire to live and luck. Right then I got plain good luck. Before the supervisor could call roll and get a good look at me, the camp sirens began to blare.

Nazis scattered in fear. The siren meant Auschwitz was under attack!

A plane zoomed overhead, releasing yellow smoke in a circle over the whole camp. I guessed that meant they wouldn't bomb inside the smoky circle. The side of the plane had a flag with stars and stripes on it. It was an American plane!

I was thrilled. I knew the United States was one of the countries fighting the Nazis. If the Americans were able to fly over Auschwitz, surely that meant the war was almost over. I only had to hang on a little longer! I also wanted to laugh, seeing the Nazis scared like helpless little children. Too bad Dr. Mengele wasn't around. I wanted to see that cool, smug look on his face replaced by the fear that he made us all feel!

The plane overhead did not bomb Auschwitz. After the war many people asked why American planes did not at least bomb the railway to Auschwitz. That would have kept the Nazis from freely sending more Jews there to die. No one has ever given me a real answer. At the time I was just so happy to see that there were people who hated Nazism and wanted to put an end to it.

Mrs. Margit and the people of my village had all stood back and done nothing to stop the Nazis. Other people said, "Not so fast," and they were out there battling the Nazis each day, however they were able.

The American plane left after that. Wanting to be extra careful, the Nazis lay low that day, and they didn't make us go to the lab. I returned to the bunk bed and tried to sleep.

I will survive, I will survive, I told myself as I lay there, aching. I was willing the fever to go away. *Miriam and I will survive together.*

Another night of shivering chills passed. Then it was Tuesday morning. No sirens screeched. Life in the camp had returned to normal. Miriam, the rest of the twins, and I were all sent back to the blood lab. I could barely walk.

I tried to act as normal as possible. It was hopeless. In the lab the Nazi doctors took a look at my swollen, patchy skin. Even my too-big dress wasn't big enough to hide it. A voice called out, "A-7063!"

My number. I staggered to the doctor who'd called out. She was a prisoner doctor, not a Nazi doctor.

The prisoner doctor took my temperature and looked at the thermometer. Dr. Mengele was in the background, busying himself with papers.

The doctor with the thermometer made a gesture. Two nurses, each called a *Pflegerin* in German, came at me like sudden shadows. They grabbed me and shoved me in a car. I didn't even get a chance to say anything to Miriam.

The car jostled through Auschwitz, heading toward

one of the gas chambers and crematoriums. The chimneys towered overhead in the blue sky.

Miriam! I screamed in my mind. Miriam! *We can't be separated!*

My screams stayed silent. It wouldn't have done any good to scream out loud, anyway.

Whatever happened next, I was on my own.

CHAPTER TWENTY

The Hospital
Barracks

The car came to a jerking halt in front of Building #21,
the hospital barracks. A terrible smell seeped out of it
and filled my nose. It was different from the smell of the
gas chambers and crematoriums, but not any less devas-
tating. It was another smell of death.

Inside the dark building I saw three rows of bunk
beds full of people. They were all grown-ups, not kids.

Their eyes watched us as we entered. Skeletal hands reached out, floundering, begging for help.

"Please!"

"Water! Water!"

"Food! Please! Anything?"

"Help!"

Their cries and voices reminded me of a Psalm Papa had taught me: the one about the Valley of the Shadow of Death. This was the most awful place I had ever seen in Auschwitz. And now I was a part of it.

The nurses took me farther into the building. There was a little room on one end with two girls a little older than me. I knew them! They were Vera and Tamara from the twins' barracks.

Vera and Tamara looked much healthier than anyone else there. They just had chicken pox and were all spotty. Because we were twins and under Dr. Mengele's rules, we were allowed this small, slightly better room.

I lay down there, relieved I hadn't been taken to the gas chambers, scared of where I was, scared for Miriam. I wondered what she was doing right then in the lab. She must have been so scared, too. This wasn't just the first time I'd been apart from Miriam at Auschwitz. It was the first time I'd been apart from her in my life.

I was still awake around the time we would normally get our evening food rations. No one showed up to feed us. Daylight turned into dusk, turned into night.

"Why aren't they feeding us?" I asked the other twins. They had been there longer, so they ought to know. "We should be getting bread."

"No one here gets anything to eat because people are brought here to die or are taken away from here to die in the gas chamber," Vera told me.

I felt another shiver, and not from the fever. The gas chambers and crematoriums lay so close to the hospital barracks that we could feel their presence.

"They don't want to waste food on the dying," Tamara added.

No! a voice shouted inside me. *I am not dying! The Nazis will not win!*

There was still a chance I could beat this fever and be all right. I went in and out of sleep. The night splintered and spun in my dizzy head. Sometimes I was torn out of sleep by weeping and shrieking. I missed Miriam.

I wanted Miriam. Then I opened my eyes to a new day, the sunlight buttery on the walls.

I was still freezing and burning up. Oh, I hurt so much! What did I need to do to break this fever?

A truck noisily drove up to one end of the building. The roar of its engine made my head pound more. Nazis came into the hospital barracks and began forcefully taking people out and tossing them into the bed of the truck.

Vera, Tamara, and I stayed as still and silent as we could, hoping the Nazis would pass over us. We were lucky. The Nazis were just interested in some of the grown-ups. The sicker the grown-ups were, the more the Nazis wanted them. The Nazis also found dead bodies in the bunks, and those immediately got pitched into the truck bed.

No one said it, but everyone knew that the truck's next stop was the gas chamber. People begged for mercy, for another chance. When the Nazis stayed as stone-faced as ever, the pleading turned to desperate prayers. When the prayers were not answered, the wails turned into the heartrending howls of those who know their end is near.

Once the Nazis had collected enough people, they slammed the truck's bed closed and drove away. Before long, the chimney was weeping ash again.

Vera, Tamara, and I slowly let ourselves breathe more easily. We had made it through this selection.

Then I saw Dr. Mengele darkening the doorway, ready to see his patient. Me.

CHAPTER TWENTY-ONE

Dr. Mengele's Plan

Dr. Mengele had his usual entourage of doctors following him. As far as I could see, he did not go anywhere without a little parade to show how important he was.

All I could do was lie there and struggle to breathe. Dr. Mengele did not put his hand on my forehead or take my temperature. He was looking at my chart. Calm and collected as ever. He and the other doctors were talking about me.

I wished I understood more German. I knew enough to realize they were discussing me like a patient in a hospital. *Here is what her temperature was. Here is the record of everything we have on her.*

Except it wasn't like being in a hospital at all. No one suggested they give me any medicine. Dr. Mengele stood there in his angelically white lab coat and Nazi uniform, so fancy and clean next to the squalor of the hospital barracks. He ignored the sobbing and wailing from the others, totally consumed by my chart.

Where is Miriam? I wanted to ask him. *What have you done with Miriam?*

The doctors all agreed on something. Then Dr. Mengele said with a smirk eating up his face, "Too bad. She is so young and has only two weeks left to live."

And he burst out laughing.

The deep sound of his laughter stabbed into me harder than any needle. I had never even heard him laugh before. Dr. Mengele closed my chart, done with me. He and the other physicians walked out of the hospital barracks and into the sunshine, smiling and talking among themselves.

I was left in the dark filth of the hospital barracks to die. For whatever experiment Dr. Mengele had concocted.

I did not need to see the chart or understand all the German to know what was going on. Dr. Mengele wanted to kill me with this disease. And when I died, he would spirit Miriam away from the twin girls' barracks. The other twins would be told Miriam had "gotten ill." And she would never return.

Because then Dr. Mengele would have Miriam killed, I was sure of it. Later I learned he would sometimes use an injection that went directly to the heart and stopped it from beating. Miriam's and my bodies would be laid side by side and Dr. Mengele or one of his helpers would cut them open.

Dissect them. He would compare and contrast how my diseased body looked next to Miriam's "control" body. Then whatever results he got, he would use them for his career advancement. For the glory of the Führer, Adolf Hitler.

Then Miriam's and my bodies would join the nameless masses of people killed by the Nazis. We wouldn't even be numbers anymore.

Dr. Mengele had it all planned out. Perfectly.

There was only one thing he hadn't counted on. Me.

I had my vow. My force of will. My promise to Miriam. I would not, would not, WOULD NOT let him win!

Fuzzy head or not, I started making my own plans. I took the anger I felt swelling up in me and turned it into action.

I was pretty sure that I had seen a faucet on one side of the hospital barracks. If the Nazis wouldn't bring me water, I would get it myself. It didn't matter that I was too weak to even walk now.

Slowly, slowly, so slowly, I slipped out of the bunk bed. I thudded hard on the floor. Just that much movement made my head hammer, and my whole body was overwhelmed with dizziness. I lay there a moment and let it pass.

Then I began to crawl. Across the floor. Toward the faucet.

I opened the door of the little room. Then I could see straight through the barracks, clear to the other side. It was a long walk for a sick person. It would feel even longer crawling.

I could still hear Dr. Mengele's hideous laughter ringing in my ears.

But would he laugh when he saw what I was going to do? I would show Dr. Mengele I wasn't his guinea pig, his child, his number A-7063. I was Eva Mozes, sister of Miriam, Edit, and Aliz Mozes, daughter of Alexander and Jaffa Mozes. I was a human being.

CHAPTER TWENTY-TWO

All for a Drink of Water

The cement floor felt hard and icy cold against my feverish body. I did not remember the last time I had eaten.
And I was so thirsty that it was hard to breathe. The
inside of my mouth kept sticking together.

I stretched my hands farther out onto the cement,
gripped, and heaved the rest of my body to join them.
Just this much work made me sweaty. I wished my head
would stop spinning.

The water, though. I had to get to that water!

The floor was covered with mud, vomit, and whatever else ended up there. By then I was so used to living with lice and filth that this didn't even bother me.

I extended my arms and pulled. My dirty fingers clutched the floor. Everything went black.

When I came to, it felt as if the whole room were reeling around me. It was so hard to breathe. My skin was sore and clammy everywhere.

I pulled myself forward again.

I will survive, I chanted in my head like a prayer. I will survive.

Whenever I passed out on the floor, I would wake up again still cold and shaky and only slightly closer to the faucet. But each time I was closer.

I do not know whether the people in the bunk beds were aware of me. No one talked to me. I did not talk to them. The only person I let be real to me right then was Miriam.

Reach. Pull. Drag. Reach. Pull. Drag.

In my feverish, weak state, I don't know how long I crawled across that floor. It could have been hours. It felt like days. I was so out of it that I do not even remember reaching the faucet. I must have gulped the water down, savoring it. I did not let myself think about how sometimes the water in Auschwitz was so dirty that people died from drinking it. I just knew this water was my only chance.

Then I dragged myself back to bed. Still very frail, still very feverish, but with some relief in my mouth and throat. It did not hurt so much to breathe.

Dr. Mengele and his doctors returned to check on me the next day. They took my temperature, checked my chart. They still didn't give me any medicine, food, or water. After they left, I knew it was up to me again.

I slid back down to the freezing cement floor. When my whole body ached for a soft warm bed, I found myself crawling again. Through filth. Past weeping, dying people.

I remembered the dead children in the latrine. Dr. Mengele would not step into the hospital barracks one day and find me dead on this cold floor, naked and staring blankly at the ceiling.

Oh, Miriam. I'll be back with you soon! Stay strong for me!

It would have been easy to give up. Other people at Auschwitz gave up every day.

Sometimes I saw the dead bodies of people who'd thrown themselves against the electric fence because they just couldn't take it anymore. The Nazis treated us horribly on purpose so that no one would want to survive. Maybe the people who'd thrown themselves against the fence had lost everyone they loved, and they believed there was no point in going on.

I still had Miriam.

A few more days passed. The water kept me alive, but there was still no food. I was so hungry. Dr. Mengele and his group came twice a day to take my temperature. If my fever went up a little, down a little, or stayed the same, I did not know. Their faces were hazy above me.

And then it was always time to crawl again, toward the water.

Two or three times a week, the Nazis came to take more people to the gas chambers.

They never touched me. They must have known I

was important to Dr. Mengele. But I had to lie there and hear the horrifying screams and pleas of the people chosen. There was nothing I could do to save them.

At some point, a voice woke me out of my feverish dreams. A familiar voice. "Eva," it said. "Eva."

My name. Not my number.

My crusty eyes opened, and I saw Mama's friend Mrs. Csengeri. She held out bread for me.

Clever Mrs. Csengeri was so good at sneaking around parts of Auschwitz. After I'd gone missing, she figured out where I was and told Miriam.

As I wolfed down the bread, the first food I'd had in who knew how many days, Mrs. Csengeri explained that this was Miriam's bread. Miriam had given up her rations because she'd learned I wasn't being fed.

That was how it went after that. Each day Dr. Mengele and his crew showed up twice to check on me, ready for me to die. Then, without them knowing, I got myself water and got bread through Miriam and Mrs. Csengeri.

So I wasn't all by myself after all. The bread filled me with energy, but it also filled me with love, knowing where it came from. Miriam was a growing girl just like me, yet she was giving up all her food, day after day. Though we were at different parts of Auschwitz, we were hard at work saving *each other*.

Now that I had both food and water and knew that Miriam was all right, I turned a corner in my fever. Two blurry, long weeks passed, and then I woke up one morning feeling different. My clothes were drenched with sweat, but I wasn't shivering anymore. My headache had vanished.

Together we had done it. My high fever was gone.

CHAPTER TWENTY-THREE

Back with Miriam

I was still not all better. But now I knew I was definitely going to make it. I just had to convince Dr. Mengele and the others that I was well enough to be sent back to Miriam.

After a while the doctors stopped taking my temperature and had a German woman do it instead. Vera and Tamara also survived, and they taught me a little trick to get me out of the hospital barracks faster. After the

German woman put the thermometer under my armpit and left, I would sneak the thermometer out and check it. If it was still a little too high, I'd shake it until the mercury dropped. I'd only let it drop a tiny bit. If I made it drop all the way to normal all of a sudden, it would be suspicious.

If the nurse had any suspicions, she never said anything. I got away with this.

Something strange happened after the two weeks of my intense fever. At night, the block supervisor came to me and gave me bread. I never saw her face, just the outline of her features in the blackness.

The woman would hover there quietly. She might whisper a little. She said, "Here is a piece of bread for you. If anybody finds out, I'll be punished."

Vera, Tamara, and I knew not to tattle. The woman trusted us, and we were in for a delicious treat one night when she showed up and said she wanted to share her birthday cake with us. Vera, Tamara, and I each got a little piece.

After months of eating hard bread and fake coffee,

the sugar of the cake was so lusciously explosive in my mouth. I had forgotten what good food tasted like. We ate every single crumb.

Who is this woman? we all wondered. She was right that we mustn't tell. If she'd been caught, the Nazis would have hanged her. She must have seen me crawling across the floor and realized how badly I wanted to live. Once she saw I was going to make it, she began sharing food. I couldn't believe she was risking her life for us.

Three weeks later I got to leave the hospital barracks! I was so happy that Vera and Tamara were also released.

When I got back to the twins' barracks, Miriam just sat there, glassy-eyed, a broken look on her face. Even though I was the one who'd been sick, she was much weaker than me. This wasn't the thrilling reunion I had wanted.

"What's wrong?" I exclaimed. This couldn't be happening! We were together again! "What's happened? What have they done to you?"

Miriam stared at the distant wall. "Nothing," she said dully. "Leave me alone, Eva. I can't talk about it."

I would not accept that! I kept bugging Miriam, wanting to know the details. She would not tell me. She was so upset by what had happened that she didn't want to talk about it.

And she did not tell me until 1985.

After I'd been snatched away at the lab, she was sure I was going to die. For all she knew, I had been sent to the gas chambers or Dr. Mengele had killed me himself.

Without me, she didn't see any point in living. She turned into a ghost of herself, stumbling around.

Instead of sending Miriam back to the lab, Dr. Mengele had ordered her placed all by herself and watched by guards for a while. This must have been part of the experiment, since she would have been the control.

Then the two weeks were up, but I had not died the way he wanted. Dr. Mengele was furious. He ordered Miriam back into the labs. She was pumped with all sorts of shots, as if he wanted to punish her for my survival. The shots made her sick. She lost even more hope.

The fact that she was giving up so much of her food for me also couldn't have helped her. There I had been, eating birthday cake while Miriam was withering away.

It was time to take action again. We had beaten my fever. Now it was my turn to save my sister.

CHAPTER TWENTY-FOUR

In the Kitchen

In a world with barely any food or supplies, the other twins thought of potatoes as medicine. I was determined to get Miriam some potatoes. But how? The Nazis didn't exactly let you ask for extras.

Sometimes prisoners fooled the Nazis and sneaked away food without the Nazis knowing. It was a tricky business, and it was called organizing. Anyone caught organizing was hanged.

The Nazis liked to make a big show of hanging people. We twins and other prisoners had been made to march to the gallows and see the poor person hanged. It was a terror tactic Nazis used. It told us, *If you disobey or steal, you'll be on this rope next.*

I asked the twins where they'd gotten those all-important potatoes. "The kitchen," they told me.

I had never been in the Auschwitz kitchen before. I learned that they'd take volunteers to carry containers from the kitchen. So the very next day I volunteered. Besides helping Miriam, it beat going to the lab. The Nazis picked two other kids to help them, not me. I volunteered again the next day, too. This time it worked.

My job was to carry a very heavy container of soup from the kitchen to the barracks. It was so big two kids were needed to carry it. I wasn't thinking about soup as I walked to the barracks. My mind was all about potatoes.

When I got into the kitchen, I spotted two bags of uncleaned potatoes. Now I hesitated. Would the Nazis really hang me if I got caught with those potatoes? Did I have a choice here? I had to take my chances, for Miriam.

I looked left and right. No one else in the kitchen

paid any attention to me. Would they notice me if I moved too fast? Then again, would it be obvious if I moved too slowly?

I squatted, my heartbeat roaring in my ears like a steady alarm, and picked up two potatoes. An angry hand flashed out of nowhere and seized me by my head. It jerked me back to my feet.

I stared into the face of a furious prisoner with a scarf on her head. I had a flash in my mind of being hauled away to the gallows right then.

"It's not nice to steal!" she yelled. "Put those back."

Those words jumped around in my mind. Not nice? Compared to everything else going on in Auschwitz, taking potatoes seemed pretty minor. It was so darkly ludicrous it almost made me laugh. I returned the potatoes without fighting.

Then the woman turned away with a huff. I wasn't reported or hanged. I realized this had to be the power of Dr. Mengele saving me again.

The next day I was back in the kitchen as a volunteer, eyeing those beautiful potatoes. Knowing that my twin-ness protected me, I felt braver this time. I grabbed several potatoes and shoved them into my dress. I looked around. No one was looking at me or saying anything.

The rest of that day I felt the potatoes shifting around in my dress. I couldn't wait to eat them with Miriam! So that night, after the supervisors went to bed, we had a little banquet. We had nothing to put on the potatoes, and they were still covered in dirt. It didn't matter. We found a way to boil them, using a pot and some charcoal that had been organized. Next to hard bread, the potatoes tasted like heaven, and both Miriam and I felt new strength as the potatoes filled our stomachs.

From then on, I always volunteered to work in the kitchen. Sometimes I got lucky, and sometimes not. A few days a week, Miriam and I would have a little extra in our stomachs. The Nazis slept, unaware.

CHAPTER TWENTY-FIVE

Changes in Auschwitz

I had no way of keeping track of time, but we could all see changes in the weather. When summer slipped into autumn, we noticed American planes flying over Auschwitz much more often. Sirens blared, telling us to take cover.

I liked to watch the planes whizzing past us. Sometimes I could hear explosions as the Allies—the countries fighting the Nazis—bombed Nazi buildings. When the

Nazis invaded Poland in 1939, three countries had worked as the Allies against them: Britain, France, and Poland. Now the Allies had grown, as the United States, Canada, Australia, New Zealand, South Africa, the Soviet Union, China, India, Czechoslovakia, and more all joined the fight against Nazism. Most of the world had gone to war.

While I felt excited about all this, other prisoners were scared. They believed that the Nazis would kill us all before they'd let the Allies into Auschwitz. The prisoners thought that the closer the Allies got, the closer we were to the gas chambers.

They had reason to believe this. The Nazis had recently destroyed or transported all the Romani in Auschwitz to other camps. Romani were originally from India, and like Jews, Nazis considered them "enemies of the race-based state." Romani in Auschwitz were forced to wear black triangles, the way Jews had been forced to wear yellow Stars of David. But the Romani were allowed to stay with their families in their own little camp, so they thought they would be safe until the war ended. A dangerous belief. When the Nazis came for them, the Romani tried to fight back. It was no use.

We twins were moved from our barracks to the abandoned Romani camp. Some of the Romani's belongings were still there, like their colorful blankets. The objects haunted the camp as the only things left of their owners.

The Nazis did not tell us why we were moved. This part of the camp, like the hospital barracks, was closer to the gas chambers and crematoriums. The rumor quickly spread that we'd only been moved so that it would be easier to gas us when the day came.

I refused to believe this. I kept my eyes on the sky, watching the planes.

In October we were startled by a loud commotion. It sounded very near. Were the Allies finally at our gates? The siren was going off, and there were upset voices and dogs barking.

It took a while before I learned what had happened. Nazis made some Jewish prisoners work in the crematoriums, where the Jews had to burn the bodies of people killed in the gas chambers. Sometimes they even had to burn their own family members. Of course, the prisoners didn't want to do this, and then they got word that the Nazis planned to kill them next. The Nazis always killed these crematorium workers every few months.

The prisoners refused to sit back and take this. Like the Romani, they decided to fight. Some women sneaked gunpowder while working in a munitions factory at Auschwitz, and the prisoners used this to set fire to one of the crematoriums. They planned a full-scale rebellion against the Nazis of Auschwitz.

The Nazis quickly squashed the rebellion and killed everyone they could find who was involved. Some of the bodies of the rebels were left hanging on the gates of Auschwitz as a lesson to the rest of us. The brave prisoners had tried so, so hard to save all of us. This was not the only time prisoners in a Nazi death camp fought back, but it was never enough to save the prisoners.

Now we were back to waiting for the Allies.

Each day I woke up not knowing what would happen. This could be the day the Allies arrived. This could be the day the Nazis sent the rest of us twins to the gas chambers. Every day I had to be on my feet, ready for anything.

Snow fell over Auschwitz. Winter was here, and we didn't have the right clothing to keep us warm. I had never known such cold before. My body always felt encased in ice, shivering and shuddering. There was no relief for any prisoner. Miriam and I snuggled together, hoping for liberation.

CHAPTER TWENTY-SIX

Dr. Mengele
Escapes

Outside Auschwitz, Europe was plunged in war. Sherman tanks rumbled down city streets. Planes dropped bombs. The air was often filled with the sounds of gunfire and the marching of soldiers' boots. In some places the Nazi hold was so strong that the Allies had to retake the area street by street.

American troops and other Allies were coming from the west. Soviet Union troops were coming from the east. Hitler and the leader of the Soviet Union, Joseph Stalin, used to be on the same team. Then, wanting more power, Hitler had ordered his troops to turn on Stalin. Before this, Americans had not liked Stalin because of his Communist politics. The vicious ways Stalin treated his own people didn't help, either. But there's a saying: The enemy of my enemy is my friend. Angry about the betrayal, the Soviet Union had teamed up with the Allies to take the Nazis down.

As Allied soldiers marched through Europe, they sometimes met up with members of the Resistance, also called partisans. These were ordinary men, women, and children who were fighting the Nazis however they could. They could be found in all the countries the Nazis were in, including Germany. Not all Germans were Nazis.

The Resistance might hide Jews in their attics, or send out top secret information the Nazis didn't want known. If they got caught, it was often deadly. The Nazis even executed children caught working for the Resistance.

Stuck inside Auschwitz, I did not know about these

brave men, women, and children. Only later were their stories told to the world. Like so many of the people killed in the death camps, their names might not be known. But their courage helped stop the Nazis.

Some of the Nazis still believed they were going to win this war. Hitler had promised them something he called the Third Reich, which was a thousand years of Nazi rule.

Others, like Dr. Mengele, saw the tide turn in the war and knew Hitler and his forces would fail. Once the Allies won, the people in Hitler's good graces would no longer be seen as heroic Aryans. They would be seen as *war criminals*. They could be executed themselves after the balance of power shifted.

While I watched planes in the sky, Dr. Mengele plotted his escape.

I did not know all these details then. I just knew I had not seen Dr. Mengele for a while. The Nazis gathered groups of adults and sent them out on marches. Why? Where to? One snowy morning Miriam and I lay shivering on our straw beds and heard a loudspeaker announcing that they'd be taking us deep into Germany to protect us from the fighting.

Nazis doing something for our protection? I didn't believe it for a heartbeat. The twins talked about what to do. I already knew what I thought.

"I am not going to leave the barracks," I declared. Since I was staying, Miriam stayed. I half expected the SS to come in and drag us out. Their voices were different today.

Normally they just sounded angry. Today they were...desperate.

The whole day passed.

The next morning there was no roll call. This was stranger and stranger. I got up and peeked out the barracks door. I could not believe what I saw.

There were no Nazis.

Did this mean we were free?

That did not seem real. I did not know then that the groups taken by the Nazis the day before had been sent on a death march, where many would be brutalized and killed by the Nazis. I just knew that after days and days of Nazis, now there was just silent snow falling on Auschwitz. Many people had the same thoughts I did: food and warmth!

Two other twin girls and I went out into the snow, trying to find blankets and something to eat. I hoped I could find new shoes, too. I still had the same shoes from home and they had gotten so bad that the bottoms flapped and let in snow. I had tried tying a string around the shoes. That only stopped a little of the snow from coming in. My toes felt like little icicles.

One man cut through the barbed wire fence so we could travel to a set of buildings we called Canada. Canada was where the Nazis kept many of the things they'd stolen from their prisoners.

Inside it was like a little store. Clothing went from the floor to the ceiling like a bookcase. I did not let myself think that these clothes had once belonged to people. I climbed on top of piles of clothes as if I were climbing a mountain. There weren't any shoes my size, so I found a pair a little too big for me and stuffed them with rags to keep them from falling off.

Besides going to Canada, we made trips to the kitchen. No more small portions. We could eat as much as we wanted!

This was how it went for several days. No Nazis. No rules. Food and blankets! Whenever we needed more, I went out so Miriam could rest. Miriam also made sure to watch our few belongings so they didn't get taken.

I thought the coast was clear one day when I was with a group of people rummaging through the kitchen. I filled my arms with loaves of bread. Just looking at so much food made my mouth water. I couldn't wait to share this feast with Miriam.

The roaring sound of a car engine caught everyone's attention. That was one sound we hadn't heard since the Nazis left. Had prisoners found cars? Were the Allies here?

Not putting down the bread, I stepped outside to check it out. The others in the kitchen did, too. What I saw made my body freeze colder than the day.

The Nazis were back!

A jeep careened through the camp. Four Nazis with machine guns were in it, looking for anyone to shoot.

Before I knew it, the jeep was only a few feet away. The Nazis leapt out, ready to take us on. One of the Nazis turned his machine gun on me. He aimed it directly at my head.

I felt rooted to the spot. After all this time, after surviving the fever, Dr. Mengele, and the day-to-day horror of a death camp, after it looked as though the Nazis had finally left...this was going to be my end? Gunned down for getting some bread? Being one of Dr. Mengele's twins was not going to save me anymore.

Far off in the back of my mind were some memories from years ago. The jumping pictures in the schoolhouse: *How to Catch and Kill a Jew.* A father and son running. Not being able to get away. The hunters were always too strong for the hunted.

I saw the long barrel of the gun. Then the Nazi put his finger to the trigger and fired.

CHAPTER TWENTY-SEVEN

Miriam Is Lost!

Blackness. Silence.

So this is what it feels like to be dead, I thought blandly. After some time passed, my eyes opened.

This wasn't much of an afterlife. I was still in Auschwitz, staring up at the slate-gray sky.

All the people who'd also been in the kitchen were

lying by me, not moving. The bread I'd dropped had turned soggy in the snow.

I stretched out my arms. They worked perfectly. That was weird. Next I tried moving my legs. They moved just like regular legs. Even weirder. I touched my body and it felt like my body. Then I put my hand out and laid it on the girl next to me. She felt as cold as winter and didn't stir.

I am alive. I guessed I had fainted when I saw the gun pointed at me, and the Nazis figured I was dead. Papa might have believed it was a miracle. I just knew I'd somehow been able to beat the Nazis yet again.

Where were those Nazis? I didn't see any sign of them. The tracks from their jeep were deeply embedded in the snow and trailed off. Were they going through the barracks? Had they found Miriam?

Miriam!

I jumped to my feet and ran.

"The Nazis are back!" I cried when I skidded into the barracks. Miriam clung to me as I told her what had happened. It had been such a close call!

We spent the rest of the day huddling in the straw, watching for Nazis. It got to be nighttime, and still they didn't show up. Had they left again? Could we ever believe they'd left for good?

We slept on edge. In the middle of the night a giant boom rattled the barracks. Even though it was winter, the whole room felt very hot. The barracks looked like shadows and the color red.

We ran to the door, knowing something was very wrong. The Nazis had blown up Canada and the crematoriums. Clothes from Canada soared through the sky as if they were flags. No matter where I looked, I saw flames reaching for the sky like desperate hands.

Why would the Nazis destroy their own things? The Allies must have been really close now. The Nazis were trying to hide what they'd done!

The four Nazis who'd shot at me earlier were back. "Anyone who doesn't march will be shot!" one yelled.

We had a choice: flames or Nazis. So when the Nazis had us line up, I obeyed. That meant Miriam did, too. With the fires blazing all around us, the Nazis did not bother to get us into one perfect, straight line. Instead we were bunched together in a crowd. That gave me an idea.

"Miriam, stay with me!" I cried. Grabbing her hand, I forced us toward the middle. We had to dodge moving elbows and bumping waists. If the Nazis fired their guns at us, and I figured they would, it would be hard to hit anyone in the middle of the crowd.

The Nazis screamed at us to march. I'd known it was too good to be true when they didn't force us to march before. As a crowd we began moving.

"Hurry!" a Nazi shouted. A guard fired shots. Miriam and I cringed and held hands more tightly. With so many grown-ups pushing and moving around us, it was hard to keep up and not get separated.

The Nazis turned us away from the fires and led us from Birkenau to Auschwitz itself. To keep us on our toes, they kept firing their guns. Each time they fired a shot, it felt as if my heart stopped. Sometimes people near us got hit and tumbled to the ground.

After the Nazis marched us to Auschwitz, they vanished again, as if they had never been there. People panicked and shoved. They wanted to get into a building for shelter. With the back of the sky still lit red with flames, I felt my hand pulled loose from Miriam's. No! I turned to her and only saw big strangers. I got knocked to the side.

"Miriam!" I called. She couldn't be too far away. Still, my heart was galloping like a horse. After months of not allowing myself to feel, my eyes burned with something hot and wet. Tears.

"Miriam! Miriam!" I called. No answer. I pushed through people. I tried to look around them. I rubbed the tears out of my eyes so I could see better. "Miriam! Where are you?"

Why couldn't I find her? Oh, terrible thought: What if the Nazis had gotten to her? There was so much craziness going on that I had no idea what was happening!

"Miriam!" My face burned as if I were still close to the flames, and the tears were running for real now. My whole body felt gripped with steely panic. "Miriam! Miriam!"

I started running up to all the adults. "Have you seen a girl who looks just like me?" I cried. "Her name is Miriam. Miriam Mozes. Please, please."

Some of the grown-ups gave me exhausted *Who cares?* looks. They had probably lost everyone they loved. Other grown-ups' faces melted with sympathy. They helped me by calling for her.

"Miriam! Miriam!" we shouted into the night. Behind us, Birkenau burned, the fires screaming into the heavens.

CHAPTER TWENTY-EIGHT

Finding Miriam

A whole day had passed. I still couldn't find Miriam! My voice sounded almost gone and pain ripped up my body. I was so dizzy. All that was nothing compared to the pain of thinking I might never see Miriam again.

I stepped into another building, calling Miriam's name, and ran right into a person. Oh, no. It was strange that this person was the same height as me.

Then all the dizziness vanished. I couldn't believe it. It was Miriam!

"Where were you?" I exclaimed. We held each other so tightly we were like one person. "I've been looking, looking, looking! What happened?"

"I have been searching for you!" Miriam exclaimed. She cried. I cried. Our tears merged as we hugged and kissed.

"I'm so glad I found you," I said. Those words could not even begin to describe how I felt.

"Look!" Miriam said, giggling a little. "Someone gave me this while I was searching for you."

She was holding a piece of chocolate!

She gave it to me as if she expected me to eat the whole piece. Never. I broke it perfectly in half to share. The sweet sugar of the chocolate coated our mouths as we lay there, resting.

"From now on, always hold my hand," I said. "Never let go."

"Yes, we must never be separated again," Miriam vowed.

Despite the fires, there was still plenty left of Auschwitz and Birkenau. We moved into a new barracks, staying with some of the twins and some grown-up women. The Nazis had disappeared again, and I was back to gathering food. Miriam's feet had gotten frostbite from the cold. Her toes looked painfully tinged with black. I told her to rest up and not worry.

Some of the other girls and I prowled in abandoned Nazi buildings. While we had slept on straw and eaten bread, Nazis had dined in style, sitting on plush furniture and admiring works of art. When I went into the building that belonged to Rudolf Höss, a commandant of Auschwitz, there was food sitting on the table, begging to be eaten.

It was very, very tempting. Then my survival instincts kicked in. Why would someone leave eight plates of luscious food sitting out? Höss was the one who started using Zyklon B in the gas chambers. I bet it was poisoned. So I left the mouthwatering food alone, and later on I learned I was right about it.

Instead, I filled up on things like bread and sauerkraut. We found marmalade and put it on the sauerkraut.

Some people might make a face at putting fruit preserves on fermented cabbage. Not us!

We also found flour and mixed it with water. It made a type of unleavened bread, like what we would eat on the Passover week holiday. Food was food, and we were thrilled.

While it stayed cold, there was not always snow on the ground. So we had to figure out what to do about water. Some of the twins and I decided to go to the river that ran at the side of the camp. That the river was frozen over did not stop us. We could just break the ice and get to the cold water below by using bottles we'd organized.

At the river I saw something I never would have expected. A girl stood on the other side, prettily dressed, with her hair perfectly braided and adorned with little ribbons. She had a schoolbag.

She stared at us, unbelieving. We stared at her the same way. All this time I had thought that every child was in a concentration camp, struggling to survive. It did not cross my mind that a normal life could continue outside the barbed wire fence.

This girl was my age, but she was a healthy weight and oh so clean and didn't have the haunted, scared look of those who had seen what I'd seen. During my months in Auschwitz, she had probably been walking this route on the way to school. Studying. Doing homework. Playing with her friends.

Had she known what was happening on the other side of the fence? Had she cared? Had her parents known or cared? They must have lived nearby. Couldn't they smell the awful stench and watch the smoke rise again and again?

No one said anything. The girl turned and walked to school. But inside, everything in me was screaming at how unfair this was. I broke through the ice as if I were stabbing with a sword, taking my anger out on it. That pretty girl. All she'd done to have a better life was to be born Aryan. All I had done to get my fate was be born Jewish. Her family probably could have helped us if they'd really wanted to. There was an outside world full of people who could have done something.

Instead, so many had been like Luci, my best friend from the village. When things got cruel, they turned their eyes away.

CHAPTER TWENTY-NINE

Liberation!

We could hear the war getting closer. It was too risky to go back to the river. Sometimes gunfire entered Auschwitz from far away, ripping through the air. The scariest time was when we heard a whining sound. We knew a bombshell was coming, and we had to duck for cover. Still, we found it a welcome sound. We knew it was the Allies bringing our freedom.

"The Nazis will bomb us all," some people fretted.

Since the Nazis had done such a hurried job blowing up Canada and the crematoriums, we were scared they'd come back and finish what they had started.

I did not know what to do. Miriam and I hid in our new barracks. We did not think about running from Auschwitz. We might run into the Allies . . . or the Nazis. It felt too dangerous.

Late in January we woke to the silence of falling snow. No guns. No crying. Everything was hushed. We didn't know what it meant, but we knew it had to be good.

Miriam and I tiptoed to windows. Unlike our barracks before, the windows here were much lower, so we could see out.

I did not see any Nazis. That was always good. Everything looked white and gray, like milk and smoke.

I looked at Miriam. *What is going on?* I wondered. Miriam seemed to be thinking the same thing. Something was different.

We crawled back into bed. The cold weather hadn't killed the lice, and we lay there scratching. I was getting very good at scratching.

Much later in the day, we heard a woman's voice. She was not screaming or crying. Her voice sounded like a rose suddenly bursting open. So full of life, so beautiful.

"We are free!" she called out. "We are free! We are free!"

Goosebumps shot up all over my arms. Miriam, the other twins, and I rushed to the windows. We didn't know if we could believe this woman. All we saw was swirling snow.

"Don't you see someone coming?" an older girl exclaimed eagerly.

I didn't see anything. Maybe the others were so hopeful that they were seeing things. Stress could do that to you.

"No," I told her.

I looked harder. All I saw was white.

Then...there was movement in the white. It was men wearing white uniforms! My body went hot and cold. Who were they? They weren't wearing Nazi uniforms.

The men came closer. I tried to make out their faces against the rush of falling snow.

They did not wear hats with skulls and bones. They did not sneer at us or point their guns at us. They were smiling.

It was the Soviet Army! They had beaten back the Nazis, and they were here to free us from the camp!

Before I knew what I was doing, I ran out into the snow and flung myself into the arms of the closest Soviet soldier. He held me, tears in his eyes. He was not the only soldier crying. They had experienced unimaginable horrors during battle, and now, seeing the death camp and seeing who they had saved, these hardened soldiers wept. Big, fat flakes settled down into my hair like a crown as everyone hugged and laughed and cried.

"We are free! We are free!" the children chorused. The Soviet Army gave us food, starting with cookies and chocolates.

"We are free!"

Our celebration continued late into the night. It did not matter that we couldn't speak Russian. Our eyes and our smiles did all the speaking we needed. Food tins and spoons turned into drums and drumsticks that gave us jolly music in the barracks. The Soviet Army opened up bottles of vodka to share with the adults. Women and soldiers danced.

This was the dance of being alive. I thought back to my vow the very first night in Auschwitz. True to my word, my sister and I had survived. Miriam and I could taste freedom now. In four days, we were going to turn eleven. This was the greatest present we ever could have asked for.

"No more *Heil, Doktor Mengele!*" I cheered to the beat of the music.

"No more experiments!" Miriam laughed giddily.

"No more shots in the arm!"

We went on and on like that. Auschwitz's days of terror were over. Finally Miriam said, "We can do what we want!"

Now there was an idea. I had been so busy thinking about all the things I would not miss in Auschwitz. I had not thought about what we could do with ourselves now.

Something I'd kept locked up inside for months broke open like an egg.

Mama. Papa. Edit. Aliz. Our little village. The sweet

perfumy smells of the fruit trees when they were ripe. Our farm with all its animals.

"What is it, Eva?" Miriam asked, seeing my face.

"Home," I said, looking deep into her blue eyes. "I want to go home."

CHAPTER THIRTY

Going Home

It didn't happen right away, even though Miriam and I quickly packed and told people we were going home. The Soviet Army wanted to film us. They had us twins put on the blue-and-white striped prisoners' outfits and act as if we were being liberated. They hadn't had their cameras out during the actual liberation, but they wanted to have film showing how they'd saved us.

Miriam and I felt a little like Shirley Temple with all those cameras on us.

The Red Cross and the Jewish refugee organization Joint came in to help the Soviet Army take care of us. Miriam and I got sent to a monastery with some Polish nuns. The kind nuns gave us fresh, clean beds with pure-white sheets, and fancy toys. I was overwhelmed by the beds and sheets. I worried I would get the sheets all dirty and offend the nuns. So I removed the sheets and curled up on the bare mattress.

Before Auschwitz I would have loved the toys. Now they felt babyish. What I really wanted was to be held and comforted. I did not know how to tell the nuns this.

I did tell the nuns who my parents were. They said we could not leave until our parents picked us up. Miriam and I had no idea where Mama and Papa were. Maybe they were already on their way back home to Portz and did not know how to find us.

Well, if that was the case, I would just see to it that Miriam and I got back to Portz on our own. Mrs. Csengeri pretended to be our aunt, so the nuns let us go with her.

For a while we stayed with Mrs. Csengeri in a displaced persons' camp. She lived with a woman who had kept her young daughter alive in Auschwitz by hiding her under her skirt when they first arrived. Then she and the women around her kept the little girl hidden under the mattress. It had worked.

Mrs. Csengeri sewed us new matching dresses and helped us get rid of our lice. I didn't have to scratch my head all the time. Then Mrs. Csengeri, her daughters, Miriam, and I all got on a train and headed east. We stayed in another displaced persons' camp for a couple of months.

At this camp I found a nearby hill that was full of the most beautiful red flowers, like petals made from Little Red Riding Hood's cloak. It was a natural garden. While I walked up the hill, I saw that the flowers grew all around oddly shaped rocks. No, not rocks. These were bones.

Very big bones. I collected a whole bunch of flowers and gave them to Mrs. Csengeri as a thank-you. But when I told her where I'd gotten the flowers, she got a very strange look on her face.

I had been walking through a mass grave. The flowers grew around the bones of murdered Jews, like life and death holding hands.

Travel was slow and much of Europe was torn up from war. Finally, in the fall, we got to Mrs. Csengeri's village, Şimleu Silvaniei. Miriam and I hopped on another train to take us the rest of the way home. *Home.*

Mama was sure to make us something delicious for dinner. Papa would stop being upset that I was a girl and be proud of all that I had done. Edit would no longer try to get me in trouble, and Aliz would finally play with me.

Maybe it wouldn't be that perfect. That was all right. If Auschwitz couldn't teach you that the little things didn't matter, then nothing could. Miriam and I got off the train at Portz, hand in hand. We didn't let go as we walked down familiar streets. People came out of their houses to stare at us.

When we opened the gate and stepped into our yard, my fantasies quickly shriveled. It looked dark and empty. There was no Mama bustling at the door, no Papa inside rocking and praying.

I pushed open the heavy door, my heart almost leaping out of my chest. The house was as silent as a graveyard. Not only was my family not there, but all our belongings were gone. The empty rooms mocked us. There were just cobwebs in the corners.

I stepped into room after room, hoping to find something. I went into the kitchen, where our whole family used to gather. The stove was gone. The table was gone. Even Mama's embroidery—*Your mind is like a garden. Plant flowers so weeds can't grow*—had been stolen.

No.

No!

No, this can't be!

I had gone home for love, family, and safety. I had entered another nightmare.

It had been months and months since liberation. That had been plenty of time for the others to get back. Dear Mama. Constant Papa. Edit and Aliz.

There was no one else here because no one else had survived.

I noticed some crumpled papers on the dusty floor. When I unfolded them, I saw that they were photographs of my family and me. And of Luci with us, my friend from before the war. The people who had looted our house—probably the same villagers who'd gawked when we'd been taken away—had found these photographs and just creased them up. *Worthless,* they must have thought. They were too busy stealing everything else.

Miriam began to cry. Her tears said all the things I wanted to say.

Dr. Mengele had probably killed the rest of my family. There was a good chance that he had done it the day we'd arrived by sending my family members to the gas chambers. And if he hadn't...if they'd lived longer...

I would never know what happened to them. I just knew they were gone. After everything, they were gone.

What do you do when you have nothing left? Even though a small part of me held out hope, I knew then that I would never be able to hold Mama in my arms again. All I could do was hold this photograph. And hold my memories.

CHAPTER THIRTY-ONE

The Nuremberg Trials

During the winter and spring of 1944–45, the Allies swarmed Europe, taking back cities, capturing Nazis, and liberating death camps.

With the Soviet Army closing in on his bunker in Berlin, Hitler committed suicide. He did not want to find out what the Soviets would do if they got their hands on him. Heinrich Himmler, one of the top Nazis behind the Final Solution to murder all Jews, also killed himself after he was caught by the British Army. Joseph Goebbels, Hitler's top man for spreading anti-Jewish lies, took this way out as well. The Third Reich had crumbled, and they chose death over capture.

The Nazis surrendered to the Allied armies on May 8, 1945. The war in Europe was over, and countries began to rebuild. What was to be done with all the Nazis?

Twenty-four of the top Nazis were charged with war crimes by an international military court in the first Nuremberg trial. One of the main defenses the Nazis gave was that they were simply "following orders." They argued that this meant they weren't responsible for trying to kill off whole races of people.

The trial went from November 1945 to October 1946. Half the Nazis were sentenced to be hanged.

There were other trials. Rudolf Höss, the commandant of Auschwitz who started using Zyklon B, was found guilty of war crimes by a Polish court. He was hanged at Auschwitz itself, in the shadow of the crematorium.

Many people struggled with the question of what to do with the Nazis. Was there any way that punishing them could bring justice to all the bones, all the ashes, all that was lost? We could never bring back what had been. We also could not let the Nazis get away with what they had done.

Unfortunately, though, many Nazis *did* get away with what they had done. Some returned to their homes as if nothing had happened. Others escaped to different countries and lived under new names.

When Nazis escaped to other places, it was often to South America. This is what happened to Adolf Eichmann, one of the men most involved with creating and organizing the genocide. In 1960 Israeli agents found him in Argentina. Eichmann was captured, put on trial, found guilty, and hanged.

After so many trials, it felt as if the people decided they had done what they needed to do.

A few people dedicated their whole lives to hunting down the Nazis. For most, though, the Nuremberg trials were over, Hitler was dead, and that was that. They wiped their hands and moved on.

It is not so easy to move on when your sleep is full of nightmarish memories. I still closed my eyes and had terrible dreams of rats and needles. Of being trapped back in Mengele's lab as his slave.

None of the Nazi trials were for Mengele.

The United States Army took him prisoner after he fled Auschwitz. They did not know that they had in their hands Josef Mengele, one of the most wanted Nazi criminals. Mengele didn't have the SS tattoo all SS members were supposed to get, and the American soldiers seemed to think he was just some lowly Nazi who was not worth their time. They released him.

Using a new name, and never once showing guilt, Mengele went into hiding.

He would live and die a free man.

The world continued to live, laugh, and love. Free or not, I still felt trapped in Auschwitz.

CHAPTER THIRTY-TWO

Aunt Irena

Late in 1945 we moved in with Aunt Irena, Papa's sister. She had found us through the Red Cross. She lived in Cluj, one of Romania's largest cities.

Aunt Irena had a fancy apartment where everything was beautiful and we weren't allowed to touch anything. She did not like it when Miriam and I made messes. I think Aunt Irena was envious because we had survived but her husband and son had been killed by the Nazis. We lived together but never felt close.

Miriam and I went back to school then, and it felt as if nothing had changed. We were the only Jewish kids again, and the other kids bullied us, calling us dirty Jews.

The kids believed a real vampire lived in Cluj, and it was a Jewish vampire. It sucked the blood of Christians. They did not care that six million Jews had just been killed by the Nazis in what was to be called the Holocaust. They did not care that the idea of Jewish bloodsuckers was obviously a superstitious, made-up idea that was embraced by people in medieval times who did not understand science. The kids still thought Jews were dirty, evil, privileged creatures who ruled the world.

With the Nazis gone, the Communist Party was now in charge of Romania. The idea behind Communism was to make everything equal so that people owned everything together and no one was too rich or too poor. Their talk about equality was music to my ears. I wanted so much to help out, especially after what I'd seen. I threw myself into the Communist Party with gusto.

Miriam and I became leaders of a Communist group for girls. One day, I told the girls it was better to study for school than to go out for another Communist march. For doing this, I was given a harsh scolding by the chairman of the Youth Communist Party.

"Well, the kids have to be good students because I understand the Communists have to be the best," I said, defending myself. "So I thought—"

"You thought?" the chairman cut me off with a sneer.

"Y-yes, sir," I stammered. I wanted to bolt. This party was supposed to make everything better. Why did everything still feel wrong? Why were we no longer talking about equality?

"You are not supposed to think," he declared. "You are supposed to follow orders."

For a moment I sat there and let those words sink in. I suddenly better understood how the Nazis had taken over Germany. Everyone wanted life to be better. Everyone had a different idea of how to do that. Lots of people followed slogans and buzzwords. Sometimes the people behind those buzzwords didn't care about what they were saying. They only wanted power, and they knew the right things to say to get it. But their actions did not match what they said. If you talk about equality but don't deliver it, it's not much good, is it?

I had been following Communism because I thought it would help. But nothing could help if they asked you to shut off your mind and believe whatever they said. Both the Nazis and the Communists in Romania demanded that same thing, even though their slogans were completely different. And for a while, I had fallen for it.

"Yes," I said, looking the chairman directly in the eyes. I had looked Mengele in the eyes. I wasn't going to let this chairman push me around. "I think. And if I cannot think, I do not want to be in your party."

He was so shocked that he laughed. "You are the most stubborn person I have ever met!" he exclaimed.

He didn't know the half of it.

This and other things were making it clear that Europe was still not safe for me.

Countless other Jews felt the same. Many who had survived had returned to find everything they owned stolen, even their houses. The Nazis might have been the thieves, or maybe it was just their neighbors. Jews had no place to go.

In 1948, the country of Israel was founded in the Jews' ancient homeland in Palestine. The hope was that Jews could finally return home and not face all the prejudice they had faced for about two thousand years.

Miriam and I put in our paperwork to move to Israel. In 1950, when we were sixteen, we sailed there with three thousand other Auschwitz survivors. We remembered our promise to Papa, given so long ago.

CHAPTER THIRTY-THREE

Trying to Be Normal

Israel is a democracy, where every citizen is allowed to vote. I had never lived in a place that allowed this. I was surrounded by Jews, many of them refugees and Holocaust survivors. It wasn't just Jews escaping from violence in Europe, though. Many Jews were fleeing for their lives from hate and pogroms they were experiencing in Middle Eastern countries, and Israel saved their lives.

I went to school and worked on a farm. Being around animals and nature helped. I don't know why there aren't more programs for troubled kids that put them in nature and let them work out frustrations with their hands. After this, Miriam became a nurse and I became a draftsperson.

Miriam and I grew up and both got married. My husband, Michael Kor, was another camp survivor. We moved to Terre Haute, Indiana. That was where the lieutenant colonel who liberated Michael's camp was from, so we followed. It was like going to the moon! I went to college, started a real estate business, and raised my son and daughter, Alex and Rina. Miriam stayed in Israel, but I knew she was happy with her husband and kids.

More than once I came home and saw swastikas painted on my house. That sent me into flashbacks. Other kids wouldn't play with my son because he was Jewish. When I got upset about this, the neighbors shrugged it off as no big deal.

Little things could set me off like a rocket ship. One year at school the kids painted Easter eggs. I stormed into that school and demanded why they were wasting food. Did they know what it was like to lie on a bed without food and almost die?

The school staff thought I had lost my marbles.

When I left Auschwitz and felt I wasn't a kid anymore, that was only half true. Now I was an adult, but on the inside I was still a scared ten-year-old girl who wanted her mama and who was obsessed with Mengele.

I decided that if no one around me understood the Holocaust, I would teach people. I talked on the news. I also started my own museum, CANDLES (Children of Auschwitz Nazi Deadly Lab Experiments Survivors). Miriam was vice president, and we found 122 twins who had survived Mengele. Many of us suffered from health problems, including Miriam. When doctors examined her as an adult, they saw that her kidneys were the size of a ten-year-old's.

Mengele had done something that had stopped them from growing. If Miriam did not get a kidney transplant, she would die.

There was nothing to think about here. I had two

kidneys and one sister. I donated one of my kidneys to Miriam. Meanwhile, I gave many speeches about the Holocaust. I demanded to know why Mengele had never been found and punished. In Auschwitz, I had turned my anger toward a will to survive. Now I yelled at the world for giving up on the Jews and no longer caring. Hatred of Jews still existed all around the world, and Jews suffered everything from harassment to murder. It was (and is) worse in some countries than others.

At night I wiped away the tears that kept leaking out of my eyes. On the outside I stayed angry Eva. My anger turned people away when I just wanted them to care.

Then in 1993, a call came from Israel. Miriam had passed away from cancer. Mengele got the last laugh after all. I was convinced his experiments had caused the cancer. I cried for Miriam with all the tears I had not let myself shed at Auschwitz. I had promised to keep her alive, no matter what.

In the night I sought out her hand with mine and found nothing there.

CHAPTER THIRTY-FOUR

Another Nazi Doctor

Later that year I sat across from Dr. Hans Münch, a Nazi doctor who had known Mengele. He was a former Nazi, and I was a Jew. But we both wanted to prevent the Holocaust from ever happening again.

Dr. Münch had joined the Nazi Party and worked at Auschwitz. While he was there, he realized just how horrible Nazism was. He started saving Jews when he could. In the years after the war, he spoke out about what the Nazis had done and tried to educate people. For these reasons, he was not imprisoned.

I talked to Dr. Münch about something that especially horrified me: Holocaust denial. Even with all the evidence out there, there were people who insisted the Jews had made it all up or exaggerated their experiences for attention or money. The cruelty never seemed to stop. I wanted Dr. Münch to sign a paper saying he had seen what happened in the gas chambers. He agreed. He was a polite, generous man. I had not expected that.

I wanted Dr. Münch to make his statement himself at Auschwitz on the anniversary of liberation.

I thought I should give Dr. Münch something in return for what he'd offered to do for me. But what? You didn't exactly thank a Nazi, not even a former Nazi! I spent a lot of time thinking about this.

The world was still so unkind sometimes. The Holocaust had not even been the last genocide. In 1994, around the time I met Dr. Münch, the Hutus tried to kill all the Tutsis and Twa people in Rwanda. The Hutus, Tutsis, and Twas were different ethnic groups in the country, and the radio kept playing speeches saying that the Tutsis were cockroaches, just as the Nazis had called Jews names to make them seem less than human. A perfect storm rose out of many different things going on in the country, and when the dust cleared, between five hundred thousand and one million people had been murdered.

What could anyone do to prevent bigotry and hatred? Anger created more anger. And I had every reason in the world to be angry. When I blew up at people, what I wanted to do was blow up at Mengele.

I was washing dishes when an idea came to me.

I could forgive Dr. Münch.

I looked up *forgive* in the dictionary. It meant "to cease to feel resentment against." So it means you stop hating someone. I had resented Dr. Münch before I met him. After I saw what he was doing, my feelings got a lot more complicated.

I knew he had been part of something terrible, but he had changed and helped. He was probably kept awake at night by different nightmares.

So when the two of us met at Auschwitz, Dr. Münch read and signed a paper about the gas chambers. I read a paper saying I forgave him. I did this in my name alone. I could not speak for other survivors, who might feel different.

Dr. Münch was deeply touched. But what shocked me was how much better I felt, as if I'd released some of my always-burning anger. I had not felt this light since before the war. Back in America, I told a friend about this.

"Well, it's all well and good you forgive Dr. Münch," she said. "But he didn't do anything to you. Can you forgive Dr. Mengele?"

In an instant I was out of my kitchen and back in Auschwitz. My stomach was hollow. Cries and screams in the night. Poking needles. Mengele hovering overhead, like the angel of death who had spirited away my Miriam, laughing down at me.

I pulled myself back into the moment. Forgive Mengele? Impossible!

CHAPTER THIRTY-FIVE

Healing

Then I thought about it more.

I had not been in Auschwitz for more than half a century. The guns were silent, so I was not in a situation where I had to fight for my life. What gripped me then were the memories.

They kept me forever Mengele's victim. I did not want to be his victim. Yet every time I thought about him, I felt his power come over me like darkness.

The gates of Auschwitz had been open more than fifty years. But I was still a prisoner there, in my mind. Would Mama and Papa have wanted that for me? Was this really the best way to honor their memories?

I looked at people around me. Everyone suffers. I especially related to kids who had problems. They might be bullied at school, or they might be abused at home. These children often grew up to be angry, sad adults who made others feel angry or sad.

Did it have to be that way?

In so many talks about the Holocaust, the Nazis are described as evil people or monsters. We use supernatural terms because the Holocaust feels beyond all human understanding. But in Auschwitz, there were no Big Bad Wolves. There were no vampires. Everyone there had been human.

Humans had done those terrible things to other humans. They followed buzzwords and did not use their own minds. No child knows to hate everyone from another group unless they're taught to do so.

This did not excuse what the Nazis had done. They could have chosen to act differently. The Allies and members of the Resistance had taught me that. For years I had thought Mengele was strong and powerful. Now I realized what a weak, pathetic little man he was.

I got out a dictionary and began writing down words. *Brutal. Vicious. Dehumanizing.*

These were words that described the experiments Mengele had forced on me.

Late that night I stood in my house and looked across the room. I imagined Mengele was there with me. I wasn't so short anymore. I looked at the imaginary, ghostly form of Mengele. He was wearing his Nazi uniform and his white lab coat, just like I remembered. His hat tilted rakishly. His boots were as shiny as ever.

In my imagination, I looked Mengele straight in the eyes. I told him all the angry words I'd found to describe his experiments. I called him every nasty name in the book. He stood there and took it because he had to. He followed my orders now. With each new thing I called him, he seemed to shrink smaller and smaller. At the same time, I felt taller and taller.

When I was done yelling at him, there was a moment of silence. I felt like a giant, and Mengele was tiny.

"And," I said, taking a deep breath, "in spite of all that, I forgive you."

Mengele disappeared. The gates of Auschwitz opened in my mind. I had finally found a way to free myself.

CHAPTER THIRTY-SIX

Flowers in the Garden

I became a new Eva. I finally stopped feeling that everything about me was wrong. The little girl in me stopped
crying, stopped being angry all the time, and learned to
trust people.

I smiled, joked, and laughed. I got to enjoy things I
loved—like Chicken McNuggets and the color blue.

Instead of sometimes raging during speeches, I

talked to people about survival and healing. Everyone gets victimized during their lives, but if people spend the rest of their days embracing a feeling of victimhood, who does that help? Surely not them.

Instead of pulling away from me the way people had done when I was angry, they listened, accepted, and embraced my ideas. I believe fully that if you are being attacked, you have every right to defend yourself. You don't have to sit back and take abuse. But if the trauma is over and still controls your whole life, I feel you have a right to heal yourself.

Some survivors are horrified that I forgave Mengele. *Look what he did!* they point out. *It's unforgivable!*

I have to be very careful in how I explain this. When I say I forgive him, I mean that I no longer let myself hate him because that keeps him on my mind and gives him power over me. By not letting him hurt me anymore, I let myself continue my life and no longer feel like a trapped victim. For me, forgiveness is about *personal healing.*

I do not say that what he did should be forgotten,

accepted, pardoned, or excused or that Nazis should not be punished for their crimes. Never! Some people argue you can only truly forgive someone if they show they're sorry. I know I'm never going to get a "Sorry" from Mengele, so where does that leave me? I did not forgive Mengele and the other Nazis because they deserve it. I forgave them because I deserve it. I see the pain and anger in other Holocaust survivors, and I've felt that way, too. If someone had suggested I forgive Mengele before I was ready, I would have told them they were crazy. So I get it. I hope the other survivors can find healing, however it may work for them.

It is very hard to be a child and grow up, no matter what your life is. So I especially like to talk in schools. Some places teach *tolerance* to prevent hatred. I prefer *respect*. I think if we learn to respect one another in the first place, this will prevent many terrible things from happening. Respecting people does not mean you have to agree with them on everything. But you hear them out and they hear you out. When all respect is lost, then we reach extremes like Nazism.

Not long after I embraced forgiveness, someone burned down my Holocaust museum and spray-painted REMEMBER TIMMY MCVEIGH on the side of the building. Timothy McVeigh was a terrorist who'd bombed a government building in Oklahoma in 1995 and had been put to death in Terre Haute in 2001. When police investigated McVeigh, they found a book in his car that talked about evil Jews controlling the world and said that Jews and other "inferior races" needed to be killed. Whoever had attacked my little museum must've felt the same way. Was this my punishment for talking about forgiveness? I was trying to find kindness, but the response was just cruelty again.

And then something wonderful happened. Children from all around the state saved up money to build a new museum. They had heard my words when I visited them. Now they wanted to help. Whoever thinks children can't do amazing things doesn't know children very well. I was in a classroom of first graders, and I asked a girl, "What do you know about the Holocaust?" She said, "I know when you were my age, people were very mean to you and that was wrong." I couldn't have said it better.

People from Terre Haute also came forward to help. They understood the Holocaust better now because of my talks. I received donations from every state in America and from four other countries. Thanks to the children and other donors, the museum was able to open its doors again.

This time, love had won out over hate.

In the museum I have pictures of my whole family. Mama, Papa, Edit and Aliz, Miriam and me. I won't let people forget the Holocaust, and I won't let people forget my family, either. Even though my relatives are not alive, I think about them and feel them each day.

I have a photo of what my village looked like from my bedroom window. I have images of the Holocaust. I have reminders that we all make choices. Sometimes those choices are little, and sometimes those choices stay with us for the rest of our lives.

And I talk about healing.

Mama's embroidery was right. *Your mind is like a garden. Plant flowers so weeds can't grow.*

I am planting flowers and brushing away the weeds. I am calling on the world to join me. If humans can do the worst acts, we can also do the best.

This world could use a lot more healing.

Afterword

By Danica Davidson

Back before my family were the Davidsons, they were the Devenishskis. My twelve-year-old great-grandfather and family escaped to America in 1905 to get away from pogroms and other types of antisemitism Jewish people faced in Eastern Europe. But that doesn't mean they escaped all hatred of Jews. Some faced discrimination when looking for jobs, and my dad was once strangled by a stranger who shouted, "This is what we used to do to Jews!" Someone nearby rushed in, saving my dad's life.

Around the time my first book came out, I kept experiencing or witnessing antisemitism, in my work as a journalist and in my personal life. I ran into people who still believed conspiracy theories of Jewish power, hearkening back to *The Protocols of the Elders of Zion*. One person I worked for told me that calling Jewish people Nazis "wasn't a big deal" and that "it happened all the time." Did she not know what Nazis did?

People in my life said things like "Oh, the Jews don't know what suffering is. They only had a few bad years in the forties." Or "The Holocaust wasn't that bad." Or "Jews never lived in ghettos." The people who said these things didn't deny the Holocaust had happened, but they knew next to nothing about it, and they kept spreading misinformation to make the Holocaust seem like a minor problem instead of a *genocide*. It kept happening and happening.

I felt a need to do something. What?

First I started by educating myself more on anti-semitism and Jewish history and culture. I read widely. I went to hear speakers. And one of those speakers was Eva Mozes Kor.

I introduced myself to her after her speech, saying I was an author of children's books. Her eyes lit up.

"I want to do a children's book!" she exclaimed. She said it was so important to talk to kids about prejudice because by the time you talk to adults, their opinions might be so stuck that they won't look at things differently. Over the months I got to know her, I constantly saw how passionate Eva was about helping kids. She could tell me the most horrific things from the Holocaust without shedding a tear, then get emotional thinking about kids in abusive homes. Beyond teaching about the Holocaust, she hoped her talks of healing could help abused kids.

———

I interviewed Eva over a series of phone calls and in person, so she was my main source. I also received help from the staff at her museum, CANDLES. They sent me historical documents, Eva's self-published picture book, *Little Eva & Miriam in First Grade* (about her life before the war), and her documentaries, *Forgiving Dr. Mengele* and *Eva: A-7063*. I read *Echoes of Auschwitz*, Eva's self-published book for adults about her life, but a lot about her had changed since that came out. It was written before she embraced the outlook of forgiveness that helped her so much.

I spent time in December with Eva at her museum. I

now had hours and hours of personal interviews, pages and pages of notes. Eva had told me her story, but it was my job to write it down, to turn it into a book. I sat down at my computer. I played intense music. I shut off the world. I imagined I was Eva, that all these things had happened to me. What had I felt? What had it been like?

And I began to write.

I would email Eva a few chapters at a time. She would reply with her feedback—a handful of corrections, or excitement about how the manuscript was coming together. "You had a lot of choices on how to write this book," Eva remarked to me after she had read the whole thing. "And you made all the right ones."

I wanted the book to reflect only Eva's voice and memories, so it wasn't until after the first draft was finished that I read other survivors' testimonies on Mengele. They painted a picture of a vain man, hungry for power, who could be both charming and deadly and who never, ever felt guilt for his part in the Holocaust. I asked Dr. Michael Berenbaum, a Holocaust scholar, to read the book and give his thoughts, which he did. I also asked some of my childhood teachers what they thought, and friends whose opinions I trusted. While they read, Eva was busy with her talks, work, and museum, but also with taking care of her health. She was having heart problems.

"A memento from Mengele," she told me over the phone, not sounding bitter about it. Just matter-of-fact.

We learned in June that Little, Brown wanted to publish the book. Eva was getting ready for a trip to Auschwitz. She was determined to visit Auschwitz twice a year, every year, to educate people on what had happened there. Right before she left, I told her to have a good trip and we'd talk more when she returned.

I did not know that would be the last time I'd speak with her.

The phone call came on July 5. Eva had passed away unexpectedly while on her Auschwitz trip. To the very end, she was dedicated to educating people about the Holocaust.

I felt as if someone had hit me in the stomach with a sledgehammer. All around the world people and news media responded to Eva's passing, publishing beautiful obituaries and testaments to her life and work. Even as these voices flooded in, I held the book we'd created and felt alone. I also felt I was holding Eva's legacy. I was overcome by emotions.

It's Eva's and my strongest hope that this book can be helpful. Helpful in teaching about antisemitism, helpful in preventing hate, helpful in showing that everyone can heal.

As dark as this book is, it does end with hope. Jewish people have suffered untold tragedies for thousands of years, but it's not fair to only concentrate on that. Jewish people have also *survived* and *thrived* for thousands of years, keeping traditions alive and contributing to society.

Before her passing, Eva had drafted a speech she planned to give on January 27, 2020, at Auschwitz, at the seventy-fifth anniversary of the death camp's liberation. I'm ending this book with her words and the message she wished to deliver.

Dear Friends,

Seventy-five years ago, four days before my eleventh birthday, my sister Miriam and I sought shelter inside a barrack at Auschwitz I. My memory of that day is very vivid. We woke up on that morning and all the terrible sounds of war were eerily silent. A woman suddenly came into the barrack yelling loudly, "We are free! We are free!"

As children, we thought she had given way to madness after all this time. Miriam, my twin sister, had talked about the idea before: **Freedom**. We wondered, could it be that **THIS** would be the day that we would be **FREE**? But, what did that mean? "Free."

Along with many others, we went outside to see what was happening. There were many people, but one group attracted our attention because they were wearing white camouflaged coats, and they didn't look like the Nazis, so that had to be good. It was the Soviet Army, there to liberate us. We went up to them, and they gave us cookies, chocolates, and hugs: everything a child could have dreamt about at that moment. That was when I realized that Miriam and I were free and alive, and we had survived.

We desperately wanted to go home and find our family, but at age ten, certainly did not know how to accomplish that great feat by ourselves. It was only because of fellow survivor Mrs. Rosalia Csengeri, who knew my mother pre-war, that we ever arrived home safely. These are only a few of my memories; it is these memories that are the source of my strength and motivations for many of my actions. I am here today to declare that despite these vivid memories, we all still have much work to do. Much of the world around us is in turmoil with hate crimes and antisemitic violence at a level not seen since World War II. It is, in part, due to the current world situation that my active responsibility to share my memories in an effort to educate the world, with the hope that this education will keep another Auschwitz from happening, feels more urgent than ever. There is nothing I can do to change my past, but I can change my future and hopefully that of others. Saying "NEVER AGAIN" is not enough. We must act with definite purpose and a common goal for the sake of ourselves and others. It is up to us to actively teach today's world, especially our youth, **WHY** respect and common decency for everyone, regardless of race, religion, or any other difference, is so important.

And until we use that education to begin to heal our own wounds on the most basic level and allow ourselves, the former prisoners, to be free of the pain of our tragic pasts, we will never be truly free. It is my opinion that by being free of the pain, survivors ensure their eternal peace and fortify their abilities to reach out and educate others with their memories. In my life, I have met with survivors and perpetrators as well as their children and grandchildren, and new generations of hundreds of German-born children who all share something: guilt. For some, this guilt was because of the memories of their own actions. For others, this guilt is because of the knowledge and memories of the actions of individuals who they do not know. Nothing positive has developed in them because of this guilt, but yet the human interactions with generations of Germans long removed from the Holocaust have been, for me, incredibly powerful and positive. I leave you with this question: **How do we use our memories today to change the course of events for future generations living long past our own mortalities?**

We all have the power within us, which we can use to answer this question for the betterment of humanity. My power from within is forgiveness as a way to heal and empower myself. I suggest that we all have the power to forgive those who have wronged us, not for the benefit of them, but because **ALL OF US** finally deserve to live free in a way that allows us to share our memories without reliving the unbearable and agonizing pain of our pasts with every spoken word or shared memory. By doing so, we challenge any perpetrator, possible perpetrator, or denier of today or the future by empowering ourselves and others with the **undeniable and unforgettable** truth of what happened here, each and every day. Our memories will provide the necessary fuel to light the way to hope, healing, understanding, goodwill, and peace for humanity. Like our vivid memories, the horrible crimes against us and millions of others can never be washed away or forgotten, but how we deal with these memories is our choice.

Let there be a new beginning which includes hope for mankind, and let it begin with **US**.

Thank you.

Acknowledgments

Enormous thanks to the following:

Eva, for creating this book with me and entrusting me to write your story. I am sorry you're not here to see this, but I hope it can accomplish everything you dreamed it would. May your memory be a blessing.

My editors, Lisa Yoskowitz and Alexandra Hightower, and everyone at Little, Brown for their support, kindness, and understanding. Thank you for believing in this book and helping bring it to print.

My attorney, Steven Lowy, for the rescue.

Hachette Book Group senior counsel Leah Cohen, for going above and beyond.

Holocaust scholar Rabbi Michael Berenbaum, PhD, who gave more than one thorough read-through and was crucially helpful with thoughts and expertise.

My early readers of the full manuscript who gave me their thoughts for revisions: author Janet Ruth Heller; friend and unofficial editor Jeremy Bonebreak; my middle school history teachers Anita English Schackmann and Wayne Tipton.

Dr. Michael Meyer, Adolph S. Ochs Professor of Jewish History Emeritus, Hebrew Union College-Jewish Institute of Religion, who looked over some of my passages on Jewish history.

The staff at CANDLES Holocaust Museum and Education Center who helped Eva and me while we were working on our book.

Dan Woren, for the support and for being there during hard times.

My parents, Deborah Peckham and Peter Davidson, who have always supported my love of writing.

Taylor Hite, who was there with me when I first met Eva, for the contributions.

—Danica Davidson

Timeline of Select Moments of the Holocaust

1933

January 30: Hitler becomes chancellor (head of the government) of Germany.

March 22: The Nazis open their first concentration camp (Dachau). Before the war is over, according to research by the US Holocaust Memorial Museum, the Nazis would create about 42,500 ghettoes, labor camps, and concentration camps.

April 1–May 10: Nazis order Germans to stop using Jewish businesses and employing Jews in government, schools, and other areas; books written by Jews and other people discriminated against by Nazis are burned in May.

July 14: Any political party other than Nazism is forbidden in Germany.

1934

January 27: Eva and Miriam Mozes are born.

August 19: After the German president dies, Hitler becomes both president and chancellor, head of state and head of government, giving him total power.

1935

September 15: The Nuremberg Laws take away citizenship and many other rights from people with Jewish bloodlines.

1938

March: Nazi Germany takes over Austria.

July 6–15: Thirty-two countries meet to talk about Jews trying to flee danger in Europe. None is willing to take enough Jews to save them from the Nazis. Even if Eva's family tried to escape earlier than they did, they probably wouldn't have gotten to safety.

October 5: Jewish passports are branded with a letter J, intentionally making it harder for Jews to find asylum in surrounding countries that didn't want the refugees.

November 9–10: On Kristallnacht, seven thousand Jewish stores and homes, and more than one thousand synagogues, are attacked by violent rioters. Thirty thousand Jewish men are sent to concentration camps.

1939

September 1: Germany invades western Poland, starting World War II in Europe.

1940

April–May: Germany invades Denmark and Norway, followed by France, the Netherlands, Luxembourg, and Belgium.

June 14: Concentration camp at Auschwitz opens, originally for Polish political prisoners.

1941

June 22: After invading Yugoslavia and Greece in the spring, Germany betrays its former ally and invades the Soviet Union. Jews in the Soviet Union are murdered by mobile killing units.

October: Nazis begin work on Birkenau, which later became the death camp of the Auschwitz complex.

1942

January 20: Nazis hold Wannsee Conference to discuss "the Final Solution to the Jewish Problem" and draw up plans to murder Jews in death camps.

February: Belzec death camp opens to kill Jews.

May: Sobibor death camp opens to kill Jews.

July: Treblinka death camp opens to kill Jews.

1943

Nazis deport and murder the Jewish population of Minsk ghetto, Vilna ghetto, and Riga ghetto, among others.

September 8: Italy's surrender to the Allies is announced, leaving Germany and Japan as the two remaining major "Axis alliance" countries fighting the Allied powers in World War II.

1944

March 19: Germany invades Hungary.

May 15–July 8: In fifty-four days, 437,402 Hungarian Jews, including the Mozes family, are deported. Most end up at the Auschwitz-Birkenau death camp.

June 6: Allies invade Normandy, France, to fight the Germans and begin freeing European countries under Nazi rule. Known as D-Day.

October 7: Nazis put down a prisoner rebellion in Auschwitz.

1945

January 27: The Soviet Army liberates Auschwitz, freeing the prisoners who were still in the camp, including Eva and Miriam.

April: The Soviet Army surrounds Berlin, a Nazi stronghold where Hitler is staying. Hitler kills himself.

May 7: Germany surrenders to the Allies, ending the part of the war in Europe.

September 2: Japan surrenders after the United States drops two atomic bombs, fully ending World War II.

Glossary

Allies: Countries fighting against Nazi Germany and the Axis powers. They included Australia, Belgium, Brazil, Canada, China, Czechoslovakia, Denmark, France, Great Britain, Greece, India, the Netherlands, New Zealand, Norway, Poland, South Africa, the Soviet Union, the United States, and Yugoslavia.

antisemitism: The hatred, prejudice, and fear of Jews.

Aryan: The Nazis' supposed master race, which they believed was an ancient, perfect white race.

Auschwitz: A cluster of over forty death and forced labor camps and subcamps in Nazi-controlled Poland that included Auschwitz, Birkenau, and Monowitz. As a group they are usually referred to as Auschwitz.

Axis: Countries, including Italy and Japan, fighting alongside the Nazis against the Allies.

barracks: Buildings that house soldiers, workers, or prisoners.

Birkenau: Also called Auschwitz II, Birkenau was one of the camps that made up the Auschwitz complex. Approximately one million people were killed there.

Canada: A group of buildings in Auschwitz where Nazis sorted and kept things they stole from prisoners. The warehouses became known as Canada because Canada was thought to be a country of great riches.

Communism: A form of government that's meant to make everything equal, so that people own everything together and no one is too rich or too poor.

concentration camp: A place where people who haven't been charged with any crimes are held because they belong to a particular group. Concentration camps have existed throughout history, but are most associated with the Holocaust. Death camps and labor camps were two kinds of concentration camps.

control: The part of a science experiment that stays the same while other variables change and are tested.

crematorium: A place where dead bodies are burned and disposed of.

death camp: A concentration camp where everyone is meant to die.

DNA: Deoxyribonucleic acid, the chemical in our cells that contains all our hereditary information and makes up our genes, which determine what our bodies look like and are able to do.

dwarfism: A genetic or medical condition that causes shortness in people.

Final Solution: The Nazis' official policy to murder all Jews.

Fourth Council of the Lateran: A set of religious rules coming from Pope Innocent III. Among other things, it said that Jews must wear clothes to tell them apart, that Jews could not hold public office (meaning they couldn't get leadership jobs), and that Jews who converted to Christianity should not be able to convert back to Judaism.

Führer: German for "leader." It was a title for Adolf Hitler, head of the Nazi Party.

gas chamber: A room where Nazis would enclose prisoners, then drop in poisonous gas to kill everyone.

gendarme: A member of the military who acts as a police officer.

genocide: Purposefully destroying a national, ethnic, religious, or racial group.

ghetto: A part of a city where Jewish people were ordered to live, often in cramped and unsafe conditions. After centuries of Jews routinely being forced into ghettos, the Nazis continued the practice.

Holocaust: The genocide of Jewish people during World War II. It is also called the Shoah, from the Hebrew word for "catastrophe."

Israel: The ancient homeland of Jews and modern country founded in 1948.

Kaddish: As the Mourner's Kaddish, a Jewish prayer for those who have died.

kosher: Traditional Jewish laws about what foods are and aren't okay to eat and how the food should be made.

labor camp: A concentration camp where people are made to work in a form of slavery.

meine Kinder: German for "my children."

Nazi: A political party from Germany that believed some races (the Germans) were better than other races (in which they included Jewish people). Adolf Hitler did not start the Nazi Party, but he eventually led it. Nazi is short for Nationalsozialistische Deutsche Arbeiterpartei.

Nuremberg trials: Trials for Nazi leaders that took place after World War II. One hundred sixty-one Nazi leaders were found guilty and thirty-seven got the death penalty.

organizing: The term used by camp prisoners to describe when they'd take something from the Nazis.

Palestine: The name given by the conquering Romans (from the Greek name Philistia) to the ancient land of Israel, which was ruled by the British during World War II.

Passover: A Jewish holiday celebrating the Israelites' liberation from Egyptian slavery. It's tradition to bake and eat bread without yeast during Passover.

Pflegerin: German for "nurse."

pogrom: Organized massacre of Jews.

The Protocols of the Elders of Zion: A book that claims to document Jewish people's plot to take over the world. While the book is not true, it is still sold to this day.

raus: German for "get out."

the Resistance: Also called partisans. Groups of people in Nazi-controlled countries who fought back against the Nazis in ways other than being a soldier in the army.

Romani: A group of people originally from India, also known as Roma and once called Gypsies.

schnell: German for "hurry."

Schutzstaffel (SS): Nazi special police who enforced Nazi political ideas.

Shabbos: A Jewish holy day when it's tradition not to work. It lasts from sunset on Friday to sunset on Saturday. Also known as Shabbat or the Jewish Sabbath.

Sherman tank: An American-made tank used by the Allies.

Soviet Union: A Communist empire headed by Stalin that included Russia and Armenia. Originally siding with the Nazis, it joined the Allies after Hitler's betrayal.

Spanish Inquisition: A judicial institution in Spain that tortured and killed people who did not practice Catholicism. While it went after multiple non-Catholic groups, Jews were a main target. Other inquisitions existed during the Middle Ages and Renaissance.

SS: See Schutzstaffel.

Third Reich: Nazis' official name for their government in Germany. Meaning "Third Realm," the Third Reich was intended to be the successor to Germany's two earlier empires. Hitler promised that this one would last one thousand years.

Yiddish: A Germanic language widely used by Jews in Europe.

Zwillinge: German for "twins."

Zyklon B: A poisonous hydrogen cyanide gas Nazis used to murder Jews in the gas chambers of Birkenau.

READING GROUP GUIDE

Discussion Questions

1. What is antisemitism? What are some examples of anti-semitism experienced by Eva's family in their small village?

2. How were people, especially young students, taught to hate Jewish people? Think about the ways antisemitism was embraced in community institutions like school and church.

3. Discuss Eva's relationship with her father. What keeps them from seeing eye to eye?

4. Why were Eva and Miriam told they were privileged when they arrived at Auschwitz? What did their special treatment actually mean?

5. "On the one hand, Dr. Mengele was the only person keeping us alive. On the other hand, he was the only one allowed to kill us" (p. 101). Who is Dr. Mengele and what is he infamous for? Why did he target twins for his medical experiments? Why do you think some of the children experimented on by him came to see him as a father or admirable figure even as he caused them harm?

6. What was Eva's vow going into Auschwitz? In what ways did having this vow help keep her alive and become a source of strength for her in the camp?

7. Living in the camps, Eva witnesses or hears about many acts of defiance against the Nazi regime. Resistance can be found both in large plans and in even the simplest of acts. What are some acts of defiance both big and small performed by Eva and other prisoners in Auschwitz?

8. Eva describes seeing a young girl going about her life oblivious to the tragedy she passed every day on her way to school. "Had she known what was happening on the other side of the fence? Had she cared? Had her parents known or cared?" (p. 160). How do these bystanders make Eva feel? Even though they aren't technically doing anything, how do people like her former best friend Luci play a part in causing so much suffering?

9. What power do words have? How have words been used in instances both good and bad as powerful tools? Think about the words used by the rest of the world to describe the Nazis (p. 191), the language Nazis used against Jewish people (p. 188), and even how Eva used words in her healing process (p. 192).

10. "Your mind is like a garden. Plant flowers so weeds can't grow" (p. 199). What does this quote mean to you? How does this quote in her mother's embroidery shape Eva's mission in life? How does this saying apply to her intentional targeting of schools to talk to students about the Holocaust?

EVA MOZES KOR (1934–2019) was a Holocaust survivor, forgiveness advocate, and public speaker. Powered by a never-give-up attitude, Eva emerged from a trauma-filled childhood as an example of the human spirit's power to overcome. She was a community leader, a champion of human rights, and a tireless educator. She founded CANDLES Holocaust Museum and Education Center, located in Terre Haute, Indiana. Eva Mozes Kor died on July 4, 2019.

DANICA DAVIDSON wrote I Will Protect You under Eva's supervision. Danica is the author of sixteen books for middle grade and young adult readers. Her books are used by Minecraft: Education Edition in special lessons on reading, writing, and cyberbullying, available to millions of children in 115 countries. Danica invites you to visit her online at danicadavidson.com.